Reducing the M&A Risks

Reducing the M&A Risks

The Role of IT in Mergers and Acquisitions

By Frank Vielba and Carol Vielba

First published in 2006 by
PALGRAVE MACMILLAN
Houndmills, Basingstoke, Hampshire RG21 6XS and
175 Fifth Avenue, New York, N.Y. 10010
Companies and representatives throughout the world.

PALGRAVE MACMILLAN is the global academic imprint of the Palgrave Macmillan division of St. Martin's Press, LLC and of Palgrave Macmillan Ltd. Macmillan® is a registered trademark in the United States, United Kingdom and other countries. Palgrave is a registered trademark in the European Union and other countries.

ISBN-13: 978–1–4039–4678–2 hardback
ISBN-10: 1–4039–4678–7 hardback

This book is printed on paper suitable for recycling and made from fully managed and sustained forest sources.

A catalogue record for this book is available from the British Library.

Library of Congress Cataloging-in-Publication Data

Vielba, Frank, 1948–
    Reducing the M&A risks : the role of IT in mergers and acquisitions / by Frank Vielba and Carol Vielba.
        p. cm.
    Includes bibliographical references and index.
    Contents : Setting the scenes – Implementation issues – Best practices.
        ISBN 1–4039–4678–7 (cloth: alk. paper)
        1. Consolidation and merger of corporations. 2. Technological innovations. I. Title: Reducing the mergers and acquisitions risks.
    II. Vielba, Carol A. III. Title.

HD2746.5.V54 2006
658.1′62—dc22   2005058059

10 9 8 7 6 5 4 3 2 1
15 14 13 12 11 10 09 08 07 06

Printed and bound in Great Britain by
Antony Rowe Ltd, Chippenham and Eastbourne

Contents

List of Tables and Boxes

Tables

Boxes

List of Figures

Acknowledgements

This book was born as a result of a desire by one of the authors to put his ideas about IT in an M&A context down on paper, and the encouragement by the second author to do so. The book developed from the original idea that IT is still widely misunderstood when it comes to playing its role in M&A. If this book can go some way to alleviate this misunderstanding the effort will have been worthwhile.

In producing this book we would like to thank all the people who have helped us in gathering the material, and provided us with experience and ideas for which we are entirely grateful. Our thanks first go to David Edelshain, Damian Norton and Alan Pollard, whose review comments were invaluable. Our thanks also go to David Rippon of ELITE and to Suzanne Peart from the BCS, for their assistance in identifying for us the CIOs who participated in our research.

Our special thanks go to the CIOs who participated in our Research: Ben Booth, Steve Anderson, Chris Todd, Steve Williams, Stan Bradbury and the rest whose names remain anonymous at their own request. Without their input and experience the book would not have been feasible.

Equally, we would like to thank the team at Palgrave Macmillan who understood very well the reasons for flexibility with deadlines and were supportive during the writing process.

Every effort has been made to trace all the copyright holders but if any have inadvertently been overlooked the publishers will be pleased to make the necessary arrangements at the first opportunity.

Part I

Setting the Scenes

1
Introduction

This book is about reducing the risks involved in M&As through the role played by IT in the merger process. Its aim is to increase awareness of the key role that IT could play in successful M&As and the opportunities that IT can create. IT can be both a cost and a source of synergy and value creation and can appear on either side of the M&A balance sheet. IT is easily forgotten as those involved in M&As battle to get the financial side right. Yet it may be at the very heart of the pounds, euros or dollars that a transaction will cost and generate. Virtually every organisation uses IT in some form or other and for many IT is critical to the business model: reducing the risks associated with IT, therefore, can make a significant contribution to reducing the overall risks surrounding M&As.

Moving IT up the agenda

A key theme of this book is that IT needs to be at the forefront of management thinking, planning and activity in any M&A. The message is that IT must move up the M&A agenda both in terms of importance and also in terms of timing. The lack of effective IT involvement in the early stages in M&As contributes to the unnecessary expenditure of millions of pounds and dollars each year as companies underestimate the IT cost/synergy relationship in an M&A transaction. Insufficient attention to IT is one the factors behind the failure of M&As to realise potential savings and synergies. It is not uncommon for IT to account for between 20 per cent and 30 per cent of the post-acquisition benefits in a merger. However, in one merger in the utilities area that is discussed later, IT synergies accounted for 30 per cent of the benefits of the transaction but IT generated 50 per cent of the total integration costs. Getting the role of IT right when companies merge or acquire each other is therefore essential to any business strategy.

Table 1.1 Case description-experience overview

ID	Case/interview description	Experience overview
C1	Large US–French group (P1) operating in the oil field services enters the semiconductor sector by buying one of the leading US companies (S1) in this sector	Parent company neglects IT, initial planning is left too late, no IT due diligence is carried out. The integration solution from parent company underestimates the complexity, time and budget required to make it work. The result was substantial delays, budget overrun and loss of customers as a result of IT not working properly
C2	Medium-size UK PLC (P2) operating in the chemical industry buys competitors in Spain (S2)and Italy (S2)	Parent company pays the price of lack of previous international experience in the first acquisition. Lack of an overall IT strategy at the time of the foreign acquisitions creates IT duplication, incompatible technology, complexity and higher costs longer term
C3	Two US competitors operating in the process control industries merge	Parent company proposed IT system for the two companies fails first time around. Large merger with multiple subsidiaries in 13 European countries. IT Integration took over 2 years to be completed
C4	US medium-size group (P4) operating in the manufacturing sector buys Swedish manufacturing facility (S4)	Parent company successfully imposes own system to subsidiary. IT due diligence and cultural differences planning a key success factor in the IT integration project
C5	Large UK PLC (P5) operating in the electric retail sector expands into new European markets by buying national companies in Italy (S5) and Spain (S5)	Parent company carries out formal IT due diligence in both acquisitions and assist new subsidiaries to improve own systems and develops a long term IT integration strategy
C6	Major UK PLC (P6), operating in the builders' merchant and home Improvement markets grows by buying smaller domestic competitors.	Parent company has a well developed, centralised and standard systems model which was successful implemented in over 100 small acquisitions since 1988
C7	Large US industrial group (P7) buys European competitor (S7) operating in the water technology sector	Parent company integrates new subsidiary with their own standard systems successfully overcoming initial communications and staff retention problems
C8	UK city council merges two separate IT departments as part of a government efficiency drive scheme	Integration of the two IT systems is completed successfully but cultural and internal budgetary issues take longer to resolve
C9	US leader (P9) in the financial sector buys small UK private equity company (S9)	Parent company adopts a 'leave alone' policy towards its new subsidiary. Both companies remain with separate IT systems
C10	Major UK PLC (P10) operating in the chemical sector buys East German	A clear and well-defined integration IT strategy with extensive use of subsidiary

Table 1.1 Continued

ID	Case/interview description	Experience overview
	manufacturing company (S10)	local language successfully achieves the integration objectives. Parent company changes subsidiary's own systems and business processes
C11	UK medium-size engineering group centralises its 20 separate IT operations	New CIO successfully integrates 20 separate business unit's systems adopting a centralised and standard systems approach. Cultural and change issues take several years to overcome
C12	Medium size US industrial group (P12) buys UK software company (S12)	Parent company adopts a 'leave alone' policy to subsidiary's own IT systems. Size and culture of subsidiary makes the integration with parent company easy
C13	US global firm (P13) operating in the financial sector buys and integrate multiple companies through its own M&A IT team	Parent company adopts different IT integration strategies depending on type of company bought. Standard methodology including IT due diligence, detailed assessment and integration strategy and reviews are part of the parent company's own M&A IT team.
C14	Two UK teaching hospitals merge as part of government drive for improving the efficiency of the NHS	Early IT involvement and role of IT was critical to support the integration and new organisation structure. Good IT planning and open communications were key in overcoming initial people change issues
C15	Global publishing company (P15) buys small UK publisher (S15)	Parent company adopts a 'softly-softly' integration approach with subsidiary. Initial IT due diligence underestimates the IT integration costs.
C16	Global oil company (P16) merges own-country operations with local oil operators in Italy (S16) and Germany (S16)	Parent company sends own IT team to manage integration at both subsidiaries. First acquisition finds greater technical and cultural challenges than the next one. Best practices from the first experience helps to reduce IT risks in the second acquisition
C17	Large French group (P17) operating in the electricity sector buys UK national operators	IT role in the pre-acquisition is standard with all acquisitions made by parent company. A detailed and long process of integration planning is followed by a quick implementation.
C18	UK PLC (P18) operating in the construction and support services sector buys UK competitor (S18)	Parent company secures key staff in subsidiary to complete acquisition successfully and then lets them go.

Notes: P = Parent company, S = Subsidiary.

Researching the area

For those interested in the subject there is extensive literature on M&As, but the writing that focuses on IT in this context is limited. IT-focused materials can be found from web-searching, trade magazines and articles, and newspapers. Unsurprisingly, a considerable amount of the writing about IT in M&As has flowed from the major consultancies as a result of their engagement with the change processes involved. In developing the themes of this book these materials provided a helpful background. However, the intention of the book is not to summarise such work but to tap into the rich vein of experience of those actually involved in the IT dimension of M&As. Whenever CIOs or IT directors in companies, small and large, get together they have a host of stories to exchange on their experience of merging, acquiring or being acquired. These are stories about what worked and what did not work; of the issues that are critical for IT and the lessons that they have learned.

The idea of the book developed from five case studies based on the experience of one of the authors. The experience of one person, however, is not sufficient to form the basis of a general discussion of the topic and clearly more research was required. This was brought to fruition through a set of in-depth interviews organised with the co-operation of the ELITE Group (Effective Leadership in Information Technology) supported by the British Computer Society. Together the IT Directors and managers and CIOs involved in the research contributed 13 cases. The reflective conversations were built around particular M&As set in the context of more than 300 years of personal experience of IT among the group participating in the project. The characteristics of the cases are noted in Table 1.1. Between them the cases illustrate the variety of transactions involved in modern M&As and the range of opportunities and the problems they present.

M&As – old and new

The M&As discussed in the cases have taken place over a period of some 25 years. Although the majority of transactions have been within the last five years, the longer term perspective has a number of advantages.

1. The business context has changed over time. For example, IT plays a more pervasive and significant role in business processes now than it did two decades ago.
2. Methods and approaches to M&As have evolved. For example, increasing M&A activity has given rise to more specialist teams and standard

processes. One CIO, veteran of many acquisitions by his company using a standard methodology likened the process to 'shelling peas'.
3. The long-term impact of such transactions becomes visible. For example, companies making acquisitions in new business areas they do not understand tend to absorb their new purchases and after-wards divest them.
4. Key opportunities and problems associated with M&As are seen to have remained the same. For example, the need for a clear strategy and integration plan is as relevant as ever.

International and domestic activity

Chapter 2 discusses the increasing trend towards cross-border M&A activity. This means that the CIO increasingly has to implement IT integrations across national, cultural and often linguistic boundaries. International activity puts a further set of demands on the CIO over and above those associated with the M&A per se.

Figure 1.1 shows that two-thirds of the interviews, in all of the case studies, dealt with international M&As.

The pattern found among these 18 cases is very typical of wider patterns of M&As which is complicated and multi-directional. American companies accounted for a third of the international transactions. This is

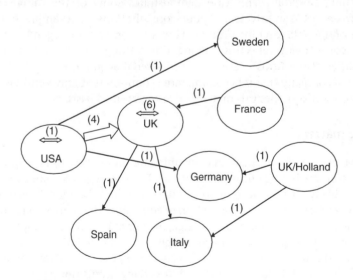

Note: Number in brackets = number of companies.

Figure 1.1 International patterns of cases

reflective of the dominance, until very recently, of American activity in this area. Four involved English-speaking mergers between British and American companies, while two involved linguistic as well as cultural differences through acquisitions in Sweden and Germany. Among the European transactions one involved a joint venture between UK/Holland and Italy in one transaction and UK/Holland and Germany in another, making for a very complex set of relationships for the CIO to manage. The rest reflect British companies in the private sector expanding into Europe and buying or merging with companies from Germany, Spain and Italy, respectively.

M&As are global. None of the cases involves Asia, the former communist economies or the southern continents. Where mergers and acquisition involve these parts of the world there is the distance factor and wide cultural differences, for example, between Western and Japanese or Chinese culture. In other cases there are also differences in levels of development, for example where an American or European company acquires a company in Poland or Brazil. However, despite the different contexts, the fundamental issues for the CIO remain the same.

Around a third of the experiences related to domestic transactions (i.e. British companies merging with or acquiring other British companies). These all-British experiences provide some interesting variations on the broader theme. For instance, one case involves the merger of two NHS teaching hospitals. This case demonstrates some of the differences between M&As in private and public organisations. For example, in the case of the NHS teaching hospital, IT was driven by a time agenda set by the government reflecting among other things, political concerns. Another of the British cases involved a serial acquirer, exemplifying a type of company that is becoming more common that grows entirely by acquisition and does this on a regular programmed basis.

Size matters

In M&As, size matters. Small companies are more likely to be acquired and conversely large firms are more likely to be acquirers. Mergers are more likely to involve roughly similar-sized organisations. The interviews and cases cover a cross section of companies that range from small to medium, to large, and to very large, measured by turnover, employees and market value. This is shown in Figure 1.2. The majority of the cases involved acquisitions; only four involved mergers. The pattern of large acquiring small held across the cases involving acquisitions.

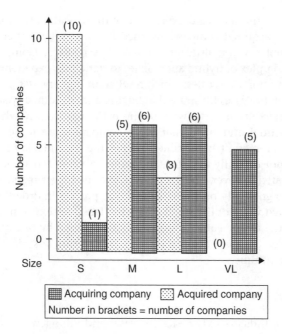

Note: Size: S = small < £100 m, M = medium > £100 m < £1 bn, L = large > £1 bn < £10 bn, VL = very large > £10 bn.

Figure 1.2.   Company size in the cases

Size has a direct bearing on the ability of companies to achieve smooth integration and synergies. In general, large transactions imply greater complexity, which makes achieving both more challenging. The larger the acquisition or merger, the more complex the IT integration becomes in terms of technical and economic risks, length of implementation, organisational politics and cultural diversity. Large transactions are also more public. Relative size is also important. Where scale supports the dominance of the acquiring company there are likely to be more options for a simple one-way integration and more opportunities for realising synergies and cost savings. However, the cases show that size is not always directly linked to IT strategy, nor are the problems and opportunities associated with size addressed effectively. For example, the large acquiring companies took very different positions in relation to the adoption of post-acquisition IT systems. For those who imposed their own standards on the companies they acquired, half suffered delays and overruns; the other half recorded no such problems, probably as a result of the skills and experience of those leading the integration. Where the acquired company retained its own systems there were no major problems and little or no synergies realised. Companies that adopted complex or hybrid approaches to standards, experienced longer implementation timescales, which resulted in higher costs.

However, the cases illustrate that buying a small company should not be interpreted as an easy 'walk in the park', particularly when highly entrepreneurial and niche-marketing companies are involved. These companies represent high value through the individuals that work in them. If not carefully handled, the acquired value can walk. This was demonstrated in several of the cases where the bigger parent company decided to go gently on the IT integration process in order to preserve the acquired value of the small company. The question of not underestimating the effort required was clearly underlined by one of the CIOs who noted: 'A small acquisition does not mean less work and less management time.'

Industries and sectors

In terms of industry experience the cases and interviews cover a cross-section of different businesses and both public and private sectors. The majority of companies came from the industrial and manufacturing sectors. These traditional sectors have had a lot of experience of M&As as a result of decades of restructuring. Among the manufacturing and industrial companies included in the cases are examples from areas as disparate as chemicals, semiconductors and valves manufacturing. Most of these companies have had a substantial experience in the M&A field going back 10 years or more. The cases illustrate the continuing process of consolidation by buying overseas competitors.

Both the European and US economies have become increasingly service-oriented. Some of the biggest transactions are now in this sector. There is also increasing cross-border activity in areas such as retail and retail financial services. Businesses in these sectors are now more likely to have to deal with the sort of M&A activity that took place in manufacturing a decade or more ago. For example the Spanish Banco de Santander Central Hispano (BSCH) made headlines recently with the acquisition of a British bank (Abbey National). The diversity of the service sector is illustrated by the service-based cases that include retail (DIY goods, electrical appliances and computers), construction, consultancy, software, publishing, health, distribution and utilities. The cases illustrate the fact that M&As can, and do, occur in any sector.

Building the cases

For anyone interested in how the cases were researched and the interviews conducted a description of the questionnaire can be found in Appendix 1. The interviews with CIOs were based on the authors' prior experience of the field and factors that other writers on the topic have highlighted as relevant. Despite the variety of M&A transactions, the different contexts in which they took place and the differing backgrounds and experience of the CIOs involved, clear themes emerged from the interviews.

Prior experience

More than half of those in charge of the IT function during the M&As discussed in the cases had experience prior to the transaction. Several CIOs were on their fourth or fifth M&A. Experience is not a pre-requisite for success in M&A but it helps. The task and the skills required to integrate separate IT operations and to contribute to the success of an M&A are a subset of the work and skills familiar to any CIO. But they are specific and experience brings the opportunity to practise and refine them. CIOs were asked to reflect on their own experience and the way that their thinking had developed in the course of involvement with further trans-actions. Lack of experience did not preclude success but it made the job more difficult and demanding.

Strategy

In all the cases the acquiring company had developed an M&A strategy prior to the transactions and in the majority of the cases this strategy had been communicated to the CIO. This enabled the CIO to align the IT strategy with the broader aims of the company. The key role played by clear aims and objectives is not something confined to M&As but is a cornerstone of corporate management. However, there are features of M&As that put pressure on any strategy such as major organisational change, tight deadlines and internal politics. In reflecting on the cases, CIOs emphasised consistently the importance of clear and consistent strategies to the success of the integration process.

The involvement of IT

In building the cases, CIOs were asked to reflect on the manner and the timing of IT's involvement in the M&A process. It might be expected that as an operational area the involvement of IT would be critical at the integration stage. However, all CIOs made the point emphatically that the early involvement of the CIO in the mergers and acquisition process is essential to a successful transaction. In all but two cases the CIO was involved in the due diligence at the start of the process. All of the CIOs, as heads of IT, had then provided support to the business throughout the entire process, managing the full implementation until normal operations were resumed.

The level of IT involvement may vary from company to company but not its importance. In some cases IT is high profile and very strategic to ensuring that key synergies and value are extracted from the acquisition or merger. In others the role can be more tactical, supporting the implementation process and managing risk. One CIO opined that in his experience, 'IT is not the deal-maker but it can certainly be the deal-breaker.' In all cases the IT role was a critical one working in close partnership with the business.

The contribution of IT to the M&A process

The financial contribution of IT to the M&A process is growing and can be significant. In one case, synergies attributed to IT in its last acquisition were estimated to be 50 per cent of the total savings achieved. As noted earlier, in industries with high degrees of automation and/or where information management is crucial such as banking, financial services or consulting, the IT contribution is equally significant.

As one CIO put it, 'the most important contribution from a CIO viewpoint is that of having responded to the trust placed by the business in IT and working together to successfully implement the M&A project'. For the rest of the company the delivery of normal IT services with minimal disruption is high priority. The cases also explored IT contributions outside finance such as the achievement of agreed implementation and operational timescales, change through major Enterprise Resource Planning (ERP) implementation and business process improvements.

Culture

IT is a technical area and one that has its own cultural and professional characteristics. These features can act as a unifying force between those involved from either side of an M&A: IT people 'speak the same language' and approach things in similar ways. However, the two IT operations that are brought together in an M&A are each embedded in the organisational culture of their respective companies. In some cases differences in the culture of IT departments involved in an M&A may be a reflection of differences in organisational culture, in others it is differences in technology. In those companies where the technology was very different (the majority) the question of cultural differences was harder to overcome. Problems arose because with the switching of one technology for another as a number of IT jobs were threatened. This made resistance to change more difficult to deal with. Business processes and management practices can also get in the way of making the integration faster and smoother. Where the organisations that are being joined are in different sectors or different nationalities there may be an even wider cultural gap between them.

Cultural differences are complex and as indicated the cases demonstrated that they were not independent of other factors such as size or strategy. For example, in reflecting on the role of culture in the transactions they had been part of, CIOs highlighted the sheer variety of ways in which cultural differences may manifest themselves. In several cases differences in size between the two sides of an M&A were experienced as the difference between a small and entrepreneurial organisation and a large bureaucratic one. In companies where size was different the initial period of getting to know each other was longer than where companies were of similar size. Cultural differences may pose greater or lesser problems for the CIO depending upon the approach to integration taken by the acquiring company. In some cases the parent company imposed its own culture and required the company being acquired to go through a major cultural change. At the opposite end of the spectrum some acquirers opted for leaving much of the organisation and culture of their acquisition unchanged. A number, including many of the cases where problems were experienced during integration, attempted to mingle the cultures of the two organisations involved requiring cultural change in both.

Communications

Communications and culture are two intrinsically linked management issues and need to be planned together. For example, 'being seen as to be fair,' can generate trust and trust is a powerful tool to understand the other's culture.

As the interviews explored the M&A cases the importance of clear and open communications emerged as vital to good working relationships in the process of integrating the two companies. However, while in each case the CIO was aware of the importance of clear and honest communications; different companies approached this area in different ways. For example, formality characterised some communications: in one case regular meetings attended by all the stakeholders were minuted. This approach was part of the careful building of communications. Initially these were all done face to face and in the local language (German); only after rapport had been achieved was video-conferencing permitted.

The style of communications reflects the culture of a company. However, the M&A context is an exceptional one and also involves two companies that may have very different cultures and communications styles. The cases illustrate both sensitive and less effective ways of tackling this problem. For instance, in one company where a people-oriented culture predominates (being an employer of choice is one of their cultural slogans) they conducted all their official communications through the HR Department. In another case the acquiring company insisted on 'one way communications' and as result critical IT staff were lost because they felt that no one listened to them. By contrast, in another case, 'respect and reciprocity' drove all their communication efforts.

The international dimension

The majority of the cases explored M&As that had taken place across national boundaries. It was not easy to extract a set of issues or practices that were specifically 'international' because of the great variety of trans-actions involved. The three areas most pertinent to the cases were language, geography and environment.

Language

All but one of the CIOs were English native speakers and conducted their M&A project in English. The number of CIOs who could speak two or more languages was limited to two. For example, a British CIO who was involved with a German acquisition by an international partnership stressed the importance of speaking the local language in the integration process. However, while there was sensitivity to local languages the use of English was dictated by three things. First, the English-speaking companies dominated those acquiring and leading transactions, a reflection of the wider M&A scene. Secondly, there is little dispute that English has become the language of international business. Thirdly, English dominates the technical side of IT.

Geography

The geography of cross-border M&As adds distance to the set of factors that the CIO must deal with. For example, in discussing the question of geography one CIO indicated that international customers tend to drive the international dimension of the M&A project. By that he was referring to the increasing internationalisation of business where international customers are key for both merging companies and they drive the agenda in terms of IT requirements that have to be met during the integration process. It is also clear from the cases that internationalisation is creating a 'virtual' world with different ways of working with business processes and operations being done internationally and needing IT support across borders.

Environment

Environmental factors make the task of the CIO more complex. Examples explored in the cases include the impact of different labour laws in different countries; the different legal environments within which contracts for suppliers must operate; or the varying levels of internet access in different countries.

The lessons learnt

In building the cases it became clear that the role of IT in the M&A context is becoming more critical, moving from that of purely support to a more strategic role. The change is taking place because the IT contribution is increasing in both financial terms (up to 50 per cent of total post-integration synergies are delivered by IT in some industries such as utilities) and in the management capacity as IT extends its operational importance. The early involvement of IT in the M&A process can significantly reduce the risks of IT failing to deliver the results and synergies expected. According to the research findings having a defined IT strategy linked to the business strategy before the merger is started is highly significant and counts as one of the critical success factors for IT. This was borne out in each and every case. The importance of clear and open communications emerged as vital to making the IT changes required. This factor is essential when dealing with international mergers where cultural differences require a degree of understanding greater than in the case of domestic acquisitions. Finally, previous M&A experience is an important factor. A lesson to be drawn from the cases is that where experience is lacking the CIO must do everything he or she can to compensate for this by becoming aware of the critical factors involved and drawing on the experience of others.

The style of the book

The text that follows has been written primarily, but not exclusively, for IT practitioners from the perspective of those who have been involved in managing the IT function through a merger. Chief Information

Officers (CIOs), IT Directors, and IT Managers, particularly in international companies, have an increasingly strategic role when it comes to making M&As work. Their contribution is no less important than that of the chief executive, chief operating officer or directors of finance, legal affairs and human resources. It could be said that the marriage of two companies is only consummated when normal operations in the merged companies have been established. For that to happen it is often the critical glue of IT that makes it possible.

However, many of the issues that the CIO has to cope with during M&A are not unique to the IT function. The technical dimension will differ but the head of any business function or senior manager will be faced with similar issues regarding strategy, implementation and management in the course of M&A. The nature of IT hardware and software gives rise to engineering-style project management which may be less familiar in other functional areas, but which other managers may find very helpful in dealing with the circumstances and challenges created by M&A. On the other hand the CIO may find that he or she is facing similar issues outside the M&A situation, for example when a company is restructuring or downsizing and IT operations have to be merged.

The style of this book is intended to address the needs of the practitioner as much as the student of business or management. Ideas and research are referenced. The book does not attempt to summarise the very extensive literature that exists on M&As. For those wanting to read further about the broader topic some suggestions for further reading are to be found in Appendix 2.

Please note that the terms CIO, IT Director, IT Manager have been used interchangeably throughout the book to mean the most senior person responsible for IT in the organisations mentioned.

A reader's guide to the structure of the book

The book is divided into four parts whose themes may have greater or lesser interest for different readers. This guide is intended to help the reader find the parts that are most relevant to his or her interests. Part I provides the backdrop for later sections, which look at models and best practices. Its aim is to place the role of IT in M&As in context. Chapter 2 provides facts and figures which may be less familiar to the IT specialist. The discussion demonstrates that coping with an M&A is likely to be part of every IT manager's role at some point in their career. Increasingly the company restructuring involved is likely to cross national borders and provide further cultural and international challenges.

Part II is intended to help the reader identify the areas where risks are located within the merger process. It is structured round a model called the Business Technology Management (BTM) model, which is presented in Chapter 3. Chapter 4 focuses on the business part of the model. The key themes of this part of the model concern the linkages between corporate and IT strategy and the way in which IT is involved in the M&A decision. Chapter 5 looks at the technical part of the model and identifies the key IT decisions that typically arise when integrating the systems operated by previously independent organisations. Chapter 6 concerns the final element of the model, management. The focus here is on the key issues that face the CIO or IT director who has to manage the IT function through M&A. This section of the book, particularly Chapters 3, 4 and 6 are of very broad relevance to any manager faced with M&A.

Part III looks at tools and techniques and IT best practices through the M&A process and presents them through a phase model. This model is described in Chapter 7. Chapter 8 focuses on the role of IT prior to the decision to merge or acquire and the process of due diligence. Chapter 9 discusses the detailed assessments that must be made once the M&A decision has been made. Chapter 10 is about implementation and the optimisation of synergies. Finally, Chapter 11 looks at the final, often neglected phase of review and learning for the next time. The phase model and the activities to be followed at each stage of M&A are also of relevance to managers other than CIOs, though the detail of investigation and implementation will differ from one functional area to another.

Part IV brings the book together through two final chapters. Chapter 12 looks at the role of the consultant in facilitating the IT restructuring contingent upon an M&A. Chapter 13 summarises the key messages that emerge from the book and speculates on future mergers and acquisition dilemmas which may face the CIO.

2
The M&A Landscape

Before focusing on the role of IT and the CIO in M&As, it is helpful to consider the nature and scale of current M&A activities. These transactions are now commonplace but their impact on organisations and the people, both managing and working within them, can be dramatic. M&As are not the sole province of the Chief Executive Officer (CEO) and the Director of Finance. The managers of the other functional areas of the business also need to understand the implications of M&As. Although many CIOs have a technical background, their role also requires them to be a senior manager and a contributor to corporate strategy and decision-making.

The aim of this chapter is to remind all CIOs, whatever their background, of the importance of being aware of M&A activity in relation to their sector and business. A great deal has been written about the rationale for M&As and their subsequent history. The aim is not to replicate or summarise this literature here. Readers who want greater detail about M&As as a subject are advised to read one of the many texts available on the subject (see Appendix 2).

The long-term pattern of M&A activity

M&A activity has been a growing activity for the last 100 years or so. Most experts agree that M&A activity comes in waves which coincide with surges in economic activity. The driving forces behind each wave vary: for example, Muller-Stewens (2001) suggests that high levels of M&A activity in the 1970s and 1980s were sustained by financial speculation that was fuelled by the break-up of companies by corporate raiders together with the liberation and deregulation of some large industries such as telecommunications. Strategic fashion also contributes to the

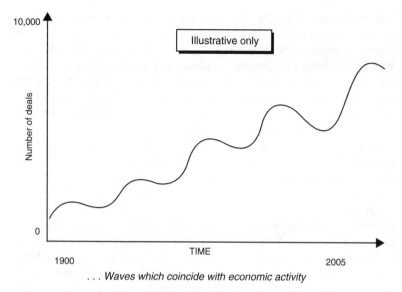

... *Waves which coincide with economic activity*

Source: Based on Muller-Stewens (2001).

Figure 2.1   M&A activity over time (last 100 years)

wave pattern: companies could use their excess cash or leverage in other ways and could grow or develop through other means. There are times, however, when shopping is in vogue.

A feature of the wave patterns that has been identified that the CIO needs to consider is that the waves are getting higher, and even in the troughs there are significant amounts of M&A activity. The chances of being involved on one side or the other of an M&A during one's career are increasingly high. Figure 2.1 illustrates this phenomenon.

Global drivers of M&As

M&As happen, according to some management theory, because the marketplace can be viewed as somewhere for managerial teams to compete for the right to manage corporate resources (Muller-Stewens 2001). In other words, one company's management may think that they can do a better job than the target company's management and therefore they will argue that they will be a better owner and offer better value to the shareholders of the target company. For the CIO contemplating extensive restructuring and tight deadlines, the notion of a wind of change bringing improved strategies and management should provide a positive slant on affairs.

However, in reality, the situation is less clear cut because markets as well as human nature are less than perfect. At worst M&As may be driven by personal motives including the chairman's ego and personal prestige or corporate empire building. These personal and political motives are often presented as efficiency gains, synergies of different types and better shareholder value. The CIO faced with such an inappropriately conceived transaction may find him or herself under great pressure to deliver impossible benefits.

There are, of course, multiple reasonable and rational reasons given why M&As are good business. The most powerful arguments cited by those seeking to acquire or expand through merger are economies of scale, diversification, access to new customers and markets and the acquisition of knowledge and technology. Behind such reasoning are powerful external factors relating to globalisation. Strategists recognise four main drivers of globalisation: product markets, costs, environmental factors such as technology and government regulation and competition. These drivers create conditions where growth and restructuring are essential to survival. Globalisation is a widely discussed phenomenon and any CIO interested in reading further might wish to look at Yip (2003) on global strategy or the work of other strategy writers such as Michael Porter or Kenichi Ohmae. For a historical perspective of globalisation and multinational companies also see Geoffrey Jones (Jones 2005).

Globalisation is at the heart of M&A activity even where such activity does not itself cross national borders. Globalisation fuels M&A activity by creating pressures in domestic markets and by requiring companies to think globally in terms of their operations. As companies operate in a more homogenised world where national markets are less distinctive they face international challenges in their own home markets, and need to respond by themselves challenging international markets. At the same time changes in the business environment and in cost structures mean that companies are less protected and more vulnerable. The phrase 'eat lunch or be lunch' applies very aptly in a global world.

The CIO faced with the discontinuities of an M&A would do well to reflect on why he or she is being presented with these challenges at this point in time. The forces involved are well beyond the CIO's control, but understanding is critical. Take-overs are not Acts of God but calculated strategies in the face of economic pressures. Theorists recognise four main drivers of globalisation.

Products and markets

Markets, whether for goods or services, are changing. Commentators have noted the growth of common customer needs, the emergence of global customers, global channels of distribution and of marketing approaches that are transferred from one country to another. Some academics argue that this trend is a result of the development of economic and socio-economic interdependence across countries and economies. Other factors to be considered are the growth of global brands and diffusion of technology and infrastructure supporting global products such as cars. Globalisation relates to supply as well as demand. Two notable developments are the emergence of global retailers and the rise of e-commerce which operates in a borderless context. In the cases discussed later in the book the reader will find examples of growth by acquisition in both the manufacturing and retail sectors.

Costs

Globalisation reflects fundamental cost drivers: economies of scale, standardisation and most importantly access to pools of affordable resources including capital and labour. Many industries can only operate successfully on a very large scale. Two well-quoted examples are pharmaceuticals and cars. The R&D cost in developing a new drug is huge and few companies can afford it. Cars on the other hand are produced most economically in very large plants with regular capital investment. Access to cheap resources such as coal and labour, for example, in parts of Asia, has led to the hollowing out of traditional Western industries and the spreading of ownership, supply, operations and distribution across national borders and continents. Globalisation itself makes possible the standardisation of facilities, methods and procedures across locations. Some companies are able to achieve benefits through globalisation in design, purchasing, manufacturing operations, packaging and distribution. The cost advantages from these initiatives are an important incentive to undertake M&A across borders. For example, Company A may buy Company B, a small company in a similar field in India, partly in order to gain access to the Indian market for its goods, but also with the intention of expanding Company B to benefit from cheaper overheads.

The business environment

Two factors are of particular significance: government regulation and technology. Child *et al.* (2003) suggests that analysts of M&As identify liberalisation of trade policies as the most significant overall driving force behind the acceleration of international M&As. However strong other pressures are, without the ability to move goods and services freely, or with minimum restrictions, and the ability to own assets and move funds across borders, global trade could not take place. Markets that were previously considered closed have been opened to trade.

Secondly technology allows businesses to operate across boundaries in an increasingly time-space independent fashion through the use of communications technology. Such changes make cross-border M&As attractive and feasible. CIOs will be familiar with the potential and the problems that communications technology possesses and the tasks involved in supporting the management of remote locations.

Competition

Changes in the market, in cost structures and in environment mean that companies are liable to become exposed to global competition whatever their location, structure and scale. Competitive drivers are a consequence of the increasing trend for companies to move their operational boundaries across national frontiers. Companies, particularly large corporations, increasingly have the ability to compete wherever they want and can pursue aggressive global strategies. Smaller companies also need to bolster and maintain their positions. M&As are frequently part of the strategies employed to handle increased competition.

The scale of current M&A activity

The published figures on the number, nature and scale of M&As indicate that the CIO has an increasing chance of being involved in such a restructuring. There is an increasing likelihood also that such activity will be cross-border. Activity varies between sectors and CIOs in some industries are more likely to face M&A activity than those in others. Information compiled on M&A activity is published regularly in the national business press. The following discussion summarises the picture that analysts were presenting in the first half of 2005, looking back over activity in the recent past (*Financial Times*, 29 September, 2005).

Despite economic recession, geo-political turmoil in Iraq and the Middle East and terrorist attacks in New York, Madrid and London published M&A figures indicate an increased activity in the first quarter of 2005 in relation to the same period in 2004. Worldwide M&A activity in this quarter reached a new level of $589 billion as a result of nearly 7,000 transactions being completed. The upward trend of the above figures was confirmed by second quarter figures which indicate a 6-month total of $1.26 thousand billion, closer to the very high levels reached in 2000 ($1.5 thousand billion) (Thomson Financial). The key numbers for the first six months of 2005 are shown in Table 2.1.

Cross-border activity represented a third of the total ($405 billion), which demonstrates that companies continue to buy overseas. Some of

Table 2.1 Worldwide M&A financial transactions – quarters 1 and 2, 2005

World Area	M&A value (in $bn)	No. of deals
Americas	641	5,246
Europe	403	4,618
Asia Pacific (incl. Japan)	210	4,894
Africa Middle East	9	267

Market sector	M&A value (in $bn)	Mega transaction
Financials	238	Bank of America buys MBNA Corp. for $35bn
Energy	166	China National buys Unocal for $18.9 bn
Media & entertainment	114	Investor group buys Cablevision systems for $17.2 bn

Source: Thomson Financial.

the mega transactions of the period include China National bought US Unocal and Unicredito Italiano bought the German bank BVH. However, American figures indicate the continuing dominance of domestic activity: only 9 per cent of the US proceeds came from buyers outside the US during the first half of the year.

The size of mergers is getting larger as indicated by the acquisition of MBNA by Bank of America at $35 billion, the already mentioned acquisition of Unocal by China National at nearly $19 billion and the acquisition of Cablevision Systems by a private investor (the Dolan family) at $17 billion. Most of these transactions involved acquisitions rather than mergers and were friendly as opposed to hostile takeovers.

In terms of market sectors current activity seems to indicate that the financial sector is the one with the largest deals (responsible for nearly two thirds of financial advisors' fees) followed by energy and media and entertainment. These current trends in M&A seem to indicate a growing appetite for new deals and increased economic activity that may create a further dynamic and more transactions in the future.

Changes in the legal environment

Increased M&A activity has come after a spate of corporate scandals after which the United States Government put in place safeguards that force companies to take a more cautious approach to financial reporting and methods of doing business, including the manner in which companies approach potential M&As. The adoption of the Sarbanes–Oxley Act in 2002 has made potential acquirers much more cautious when contemplating an acquisition and this is reflected in the amount and rigour of the due diligence process in the new M&A transactions.

The Act requires CEOs and CFOs to certify personally the accuracy of their companies' financial statements. These certifications also apply to the financial results of acquired businesses. As a result companies have generally insisted on doing due diligence earlier in the transaction process and integrating businesses as fully as possible after the closing of the M&A transaction. The results of these changes have inevitably affected US companies and delayed the closing of some M&A transactions.

From a CIO's viewpoint the Sarbanes–Oxley Act has significant implications (particularly if he/she works for a US company) as the M&A due diligence process requires a more detailed analysis of the IT systems controls, security and reporting features. In a recent consulting assignment one of the authors saw this problem first hand when the client company's intended acquisition had to be delayed because of additional checks that were necessary to make sure that the intended target was compliant with Sarbanes–Oxley requirements.

M&As in the IT sector

The CIO needs to be aware not only of M&A activity in general, and in his or her business sector in particular, but also in the IT industry itself. The restructuring of key suppliers has an impact on their business customers.

In 2000 there was a dramatic increase in the number of M&A deals in the IT services sector signalling perhaps the maturing of the IT sector and a change in the pattern of M&A activity in the IT sector which is still being consolidated. Previously the sector was viewed as a fast growing area encouraging multiplication of players helped by inflated stock prices. From a total of $3.5 billion M&A in this sector in 1999 the top six M&A transactions alone in this sector accounted for $28 billion in 2000 (Vermeulen 2000).

These M&A transactions (see Table 2.2) not only represented a huge M&A value but also signalled a strategic shift towards globalisation as companies sought the critical mass needed in order to compete in world markets, in particular the two main world markets for IT; US and Europe. Five out of the six transactions were cross-border and in three out of the five geographical expansion was centred in Europe (Vermeulen 2000).

Table 2.2 Top M&A transactions in IT services, 2000 ($bn)

Target name	Country	Acquirer name	Country	Target value
pdv Unternhemen	Germany	Logica	Netherlands	0.5
Origin	Netherlands	Atos	Netherlands	3.3
Admiral	UK	CMG	UK	2.2
Debhis Systemhaus	Germany	Deutsche Telekom	Germany	5.4
LHS Grooup	US	Sema Group	UK	4.3
Ernst & Young	US	Cap Gemini	France	11.8

Source: BNP Paribas.

Table 2.3 Key drivers of main M&A IT services transactions, 2000

Transaction	1	2	3	4	5	6
All-in share transaction	√	√		√	√	
Geographic expansion	√	√		√	√	√
European coverage				√	√	√
Access to US market		√	√			
Strengthen/diversify sector exposure	√	√	√	√	√	√
Acquisition of advisory services	√					√

Notes: 1: Cap Gemini/E&Y; 2: Sema LHS; 3: Debi Systemhaus/DT; 4: CMG Admiral; 5: Atos Origin; 6: Logica pdv.

Source: BNP Paribas.

Apart from geographic expansion, the key drivers for these global players have been access to new markets; strengthening or diversification of sector exposure; the ability to offer a wider range of services; and IT divestment from former industrial groups. For example, Daimler Chrysler and Philips floated their respective internal IT departments off as Debis Systemhaus and Origin. In turn these were bought by Deutsche Telekom and Atos who were seeking to expand and diversify their own portfolios by purchasing complementary service providers (see Table 2.3). The Cap Gemini/Ernst & Young transaction illustrates the attraction between consulting firms and suppliers of IT services; a pattern followed widely since.

A new pattern of consolidation and change followed the collapse of Enron. Arthur Andersen's role in Enron's demise sent shock waves into the consulting advisory firms. Arthur Andersen themselves were split and sold to various competitors. The role of the US Securities and Exchange Commission (SEC) in drawing a distinction between business and accountancy consulting accelerated the M&A tide among management consulting and computer firms. For example in 2002 IBM acquired PWC's consulting business after a failed attempt by HP to buy PWC. In the same year KPMG business consulting practices were bought by Atos/Origin. In the software business the recent trend has also been one of consolidation. In 2003 the acquisition of JD Edwards (ERP software company) by one of its main competitors Peoplesoft prompted a successful hostile bid by Oracle two years later. Oracle's appetite for acquisitions seems to be gathering momentum with the recent acquisition of Siebel, a leader in Customer Resource Management (CRM) systems for $6 billion. Mega mergers in the IT sector are forecast to continue. In 2004 Microsoft and SAP confirmed that they had had merger talks. These were subsequently abandoned but demonstrate that Microsoft is edging into the ERP market through recent purchases such as Great Plains Software and Navision. In the telecommunications sector a similar pattern can be seen. In the US in 2004, Sprint merged with Nextel and Cingular Wireless was acquired by AT&T. In Europe the UK carrier Cable & Wireless acquired the independent telephone carrier Energis for an undisclosed sum believed to be around £780 million to create the UK's second largest fixed-line operator. At the time of writing (2005) Spanish main telephone carrier Telefonica has just announced the acquisition of O2 from the UK for a sum of £17, 7 billion so the list keeps growing.

The implications of these M&As for the CIO are profound because they alter the competitive landscape in the IT industry. Recent reports of computer users being alarmed about the loss of support to their previous systems by the HP/Compaq merger and the Oracle acquisition of Peoplesoft/JD Edwards are only two examples of this shifting supplier power phenomenon. As will be discussed later in the book, the CIO must be ready for these changes that are a potential threat as well as an opportunity to the way that he/she supports the internal customer.

Predictions for the future

Some analysts believe that M&A activity is a strategic tool in all economic conditions (Mitchell and Capron 2003). This implies that even during economic slowdown M&A business is good business. For example, for strong firms, buying struggling companies represent opportunities to grow product lines and extend operations. For other companies mergers provide an opportunity to change the terms of competition in their industry while competitors focus on traditional operations (ibid.). An example of a persistent acquisitions strategy is Cisco Systems that every year makes several acquisitions almost irrespective of the economic climate.

Although economic conditions may vary from time to time due to major forces in the world's socio-political and economic systems, some drivers will continue as before. For example globalisation is likely to continue to drive M&A activity. The potential threat of trade wars between US and Europe and the raising of tariffs will not stop the drive for further economic expansion through globalisation of trade. The need for cost reduction and growth will make companies continue to search for cheaper means of production and new markets.

The size of companies will continue to be a driver fuelled by the need to compete in global markets and against companies of ever bigger size. Hence, the mega-deals of the 1990s and 2000 are likely to be repeated at periods in the future. The mega-deals such as AOL-Time Warner and Exxon and Mobil may be difficult to repeat but a SAP–Microsoft merger or similar is not unthinkable. The consolidation undertaken in some industries since the year 2000 is likely to continue in others such as banking, media, retailing and telecommunications. Recent M&A activity in the financial sector shows that not only banks are exposed but stock exchanges too. The London and New York exchanges have both been under M&A merger scrutiny.

According to industry analysts worldwide IT spending will grow around 5.9 per cent per annum through 2009 to reach $1.34 trillion from $1.06 this year (IDC 2005). This rate is a distant number compared to double-digit growth in the late 1990s but it is as a consequence of the industry maturing and remains a healthy indicator for the future. According to IDC this growth will come from demand in traditionally strong users of IT such as government, manufacturing and banking as well as from newer sectors such as healthcare, media and communications and consumer industries. Growth, changing patterns of demand and technological advances can all give rise to M&A activity.

From a CIO's viewpoint the word is to be vigilant and prepared. The IT service supplier landscape will continue to change and further M&A activity is expected. The industry analyst Gartner predicts that 30–40 per cent of the minor IT players will be acquired sooner or later (IDC 2005). Historically, M&A waves have been getting longer in duration, lasting 15 years or more. The current wave started in 1990. It may have even longer cycles than those that have gone before given the drivers of activity that have been identified as fuelling it. In the future the level of M&A activity will be likely to fluctuate following major world economic, political, social and technological events but most analysts tend to agree that the international M&A market is here to stay. If this turns out to be the case, it seems sensible to review the experience so far and be preparing for the future.

Part II
Implementation Issues

3

The Business, Technology and Management Model

There is a general consensus among business leaders, analysts and managers that M&As frequently do not create as much value as originally intended. Some of this shortfall can be blamed on over-optimism by the initiators of an M&A in an attempt to promote the worth of the deal. An examination of the deal may demonstrate that it was based on faulty logic and the intended value creation based on hope rather than reality. However, a considerable part of the shortfall often arises from poor execution of the details of the deal, in particular the post-merger integration of the organisations involved.

Throughout this book we argue that reducing the inherent IT risks in an M&A project is about anticipating and preparing a response to the various business, technical and management issues to be encountered by the CIO. In this chapter we would like to discuss some ideas for reducing these risks by looking at the key success factors that the CIO should pursue in relation to an M&A, and the best practices that can help to reduce the shortfall in value creation and reduce the risks inherent in the transaction.

Later in the book the discussion focuses upon the role that IT plays in the different stages of the overall M&A process and the tasks and challenges facing the CIO from pre- to post-merger. In the discussion that follows here, the issues facing the CIO are grouped using a framework which we have called the Business, Technology and Management (BTM) Model: B for business; T for technology; and M for management (see Figure 3.1). These three sets of issues call for the CIO to possess and exercise three very different sets of skills and to play three different, and at times conflicting, roles within the M&A process.

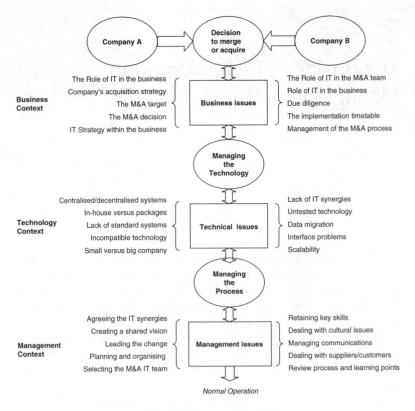

Figure 3.1   The BTM model

The shape of the BTM model differs at different stages of the M&A process. For example, the Business issues dominate the early stages of deal making and planning; Technology and Management dominate the later stages of planning and implementation. However, all three are present all the time and part of the challenge the CIO faces is to keep them in balance and to understand how each is impacting the particular task that is being undertaken at a particular stage of the M&A.

The business context

Research evidence points to the fact that CEOs shy away from technology issues when approaching an M&A transaction. In most cases the CEO's expectations about IT and the CIO's involvement have to do with this view of the relevance of technology. Generally the CEO's expectations about IT in an M&A situation relate to economic factors such as, how much will it cost to integrate IT?; risk factors such as, what happens if IT fails during the M&A integration?, and with political factors such as, what happens if the proposed IT solution is not accepted by the combined organisation?

The CIO heads only one functional area of the business. However central IT is to the operations of the company, there are other functional areas to be considered in an M&A. The initiation and early stages of the transaction are almost invariably dominated by the financial function. The pace of business M&A normally dictates the pace of IT activity. Hence IT concerns will rarely dictate the business timetable.

On the other hand, the decisions taken at the earliest stages of the M&A processes provide the framework and the constraints within which the CIO must deliver results at the end of the day. The challenge facing the CIO is to ensure that, while recognising the wider business agenda, IT is consulted at the early stages of the process and is able to influence decisions that impact on the work of IT.

The CIO's ability to handle the broader business context effectively will depend on the position of IT in the organisation. This is not simply a question of the importance of IT to the business processes, but more broadly of its role and reputation. IT is more likely to be involved in the strategic decisions regarding the business where it is well-thought of, and working well with the rest of the business. In turn, where this is the case, IT is more likely to be part of the business team that explores M&A opportunities, selects targets and makes bids. Only a minority of CIOs achieve this and are less likely to do so in small and medium-sized companies. Only three of the CIOs interviewed had reached this level. If the CIO is not part of the strategic management team, it is likely he or she will be left out of direct involvement with the initial M&A strategy and scanning process. There is also no reason why a skilled CIO should not be seen as the natural leader of the M&A project on behalf of the organisation.

To be in the favourable position achieved by a few when an M&A moves onto the agenda requires the CIO to act effectively as an advocate for his or her area of the business. A key factor is for the CIO to do an outstanding job in communicating with the Board. CIOs must talk in business terms and not hide behind technology; they may be faced with senior directors who lack an appreciation of IT. Unless the CIO is able to speak in a language that the Board understands, IT risks not being trusted or seen as a business partner by senior management, both of which are essential attributes for being included in any major strategic decision such as an M&A.

Being in a position to undertake an M&A effectively also requires the IT function to be organised in a strategic fashion. Even before the M&A is announced, the level of synergy between the business strategy and the IT strategy is highly significant. In the absence of an IT strategy or if an IT strategy is not linked to the business strategy, it is impossible for the CIO to conduct an effective due diligence or to know how to approach the acquisition.

In Chapter 4 we discuss the top ten aspects of the business context that impact the subsequent success or failure of IT integration in relation to an M&A. These include the level of experience that the business can draw upon; the M&A decision, the role of IT and way the M&A process is managed at the level of the organisation.

The technical context

The CIO is responsible for ensuring that the technical issues relating to the integration of the two companies that are coming together are identified and that efficient and effective technical solutions are adopted. Much will depend on the size of the transaction as to whether the CIO has a hands-on role in the technical issues that emerge. However, even in a very large transaction where the CIO is operating at a much higher level he or she must have the technical knowledge and competence to endorse recommendations from technical specialists. In addition he or she needs to be able to recognise where specialist technical help needs to be brought in.

The technical issues in an M&A are particularly challenging because by definition they involve bringing together disparate systems. The systems involved can be as different as it is possible to be on any number of dimensions – architecture, suppliers, organisation, and function. Integration is usually expected to deliver not only a functioning IT system for both companies but improvements and savings. Two very different factors contribute to achieving this. First, it is easier to tackle the integration issue if the parent company has a clear IT strategy and plans and well-documented systems. It is a bonus if the acquired or merged company brings the same level of systems organisation and management, but at a minimum level the CIO should be able to be confident of the thrust and work of his or her own department. Secondly, integration of disparate systems calls for innovation, creativity and new ways of dealing with technical issues. Every M&A is unique and the CIO must be prepared to help the integration team to use its experience and expertise in new ways and to come to grips rapidly with new processes and ideas.

Chapter 5 looks at the ten key technical issues that the CIO may face in handling a M&A. They all pose the need for the CIO to take technical decisions for which he or she needs to have the requisite knowledge and understanding. The success or failure to deal with such technical matters is highly visible and the reputation risk to the CIO and IT function of failure to deliver IT support to the rest of the business is significant. IT is also an expensive function particularly with respect to capital investment. Poor decisions can turn proposed cost savings into added integration costs.

The management context

The CIO bears the responsibility for managing the IT function through an M&A. This requires extended management skills and capabilities beyond those needed to run the function in a steady state. The CIO has to provide leadership to a major management of change process in both organisations. Among the tasks that the CIO will face is the need to create a shared vision across the two companies and aligning forces of influence in the two companies behind this vision. The integration needs to be designed and planned and project managed to a high level. A number of different teams need to be set up and tasked with carrying out the IT aspects of the merger. A range of key relationships need to be developed and maintained including those with customers, suppliers, users, senior management and the staff of the IT function. Finally the CIO needs to maintain motivation and commitment on the part of staff while at the same time both re-organising and often slimming down, the workforce.

The CIO also needs another skill that is characteristic of an M&A change project – that of cultural sensitivity. The organisational cultures of the two organisations which are involved in the M&A will almost certainly differ. The CIO needs to understand both cultures and facilitate the emergence of a shared culture for the new organisation. Increasingly this involves working across national boundaries. The CIO needs to find ways to work with organisations where customs, laws, language and the expectations of companies by workers and vice versa differ significantly.

Chapter 6 discusses and illustrates some of the management dilemmas that face a CIO during a M&A. Included in the discussion is the importance of learning from experience. One of the issues the business as a whole faces to which the CIO must contribute at a strategic level is either lack of experience or failure to utilise experience in the M&A field when contemplating a transaction. Capturing experience and learning from it is also an essential aspect of the successful CIO's approach to management.

In all three areas, business, technology and management, the CIO may have to deal with circumstances that make it difficult to achieve the ideal. Common problems include:

- Unplanned and unexpected events
- Secrecy
- Hostility
- Very tight deadlines
- Lack of information
- Lack of resource

Knowledge of the ideal can be helpful to the CIO in terms of effort to optimise the situation and also in terms of prioritising. However, at the end of the day the CIO, or other senior manager or functional head, may have to opt for the least worst rather than the best approach to handling the M&A.

4
The Business Context

The business context for the CIO is crucial because it is rarely the IT function that is taking the lead and dictating the pace of the M&A. However significant the impact on IT, and however central IT is to the organisation, M&A is about corporate growth and corporate decision-making. Issues such as a clear M&A strategy within the company, targeting the right company, and selecting the right mergers and acquisition team have all been identified as success factors both for the M&A as a whole and also for IT. Absence of these factors adds to the risk that the M&A will fail to deliver the value set for the transaction. Although these are success factors at the level of the firm or organisation, they impact directly the CIO's ability to deliver the objectives of the integration. They are therefore contextual factors that the CIO must be aware of and understand as they will have implications for IT and will affect the CIO's freedom of operation during the M&A process.

M&As involve both risk and opportunity for IT. The risks that are involved are primarily twofold:

1. The risk that the planned IT synergies and cost saving will not be recognised, pursued or realised.
2. The risk that synergies and savings elsewhere will not be recognised, pursued or realised because of IT factors.

Our research based on the CIO interviews, the case studies and existing published literature all point out that best way to reduce the IT risks and to maximise the opportunities associated with M&As is to avoid a number of recognised pitfalls. This chapter looks at some of the aspects of the business context which pose risks for IT and the CIO during the IT M&A

Box 4.1   Top 10 business issues

1. The role of IT in the business
2. The company's acquisition strategy
3. The M&A target
4. The M&A decision
5. IT strategy within the business
6. The role of IT in the M&A team
7. Due diligence
8. The implementation timetable
9. Management of the M&A process
10. Prior M&A experience

---

integration project. The issues discussed are the top 10 features of the business context that emerged from the cases and interviews with CIOs. They fall naturally into two groups:

1. Factors which determine the level of risk that relates to IT in an M&A (issues 1–4).
2. Factors related to IT that can mitigate risk in the M&A decision (issues 5–10).

The top ten factors are listed in Box 4.1.

The role of IT in the business

Increasingly organisations rely heavily on IT to deliver their daily operations and business functions. In most industries business will experience severe disruption or come to a grinding halt if IT stops working. In industries such as retail, banking and travel, to mention a few, the number of customers affected by an IT glitch can often be expressed in hundreds of thousands. Graphic illustrations of this are press pictures of an airport when the computer system has gone down resulting in long queues and angry customers sitting in every available space. In industries such as manufacturing, process and recruitment the products and services would cost much more to be delivered to the end customer if IT was not used. The heavy dependence on IT that this creates means that output will be severely disrupted if systems are not working. In the knowledge sector such as consultancy the effect of IT systems not working can be very serious indeed if information is lost or corrupted.

In the merger of Glaxo and Smith Kline Beecham a spokesman is quoted as saying: 'in a knowledge-intensive business such as ours, the potential losses of not having an email system could have been as high as £1 million per day' (Ranger 2001). The operational impact of IT in organisations today is generally well understood by most CEOs. However, IT can also have a strategic impact because it affects not only internal operations but also external ones. In the example of a retail company's recent acquisition the financial costs of their IT systems not functioning in their stores was quantified as £5 million per day.

Another reason why IT becomes strategic in an M&A scenario is the actual costs involved. In the GSKB merger mentioned before, the costs of linking their IT systems were reported to be £3 million (Ranger 2001). In our own experience they have ranged from £300,000 to several millions. However, these are only the initial integration costs. The costs of making the wrong strategic choice on hardware, software, networks or people can be much more substantial amounting to hundred of millions. In an IBM technical paper (Gulati 2002) the author shows that the right strategic choice of IT infrastructure alone can make savings of at least 20 per cent of the business's combined total IT expenditure. In this example it would represent $200–225 million per annum.

Banking is a further example where IT integration is vital both for customers and for shareholders. Lloyds and TSB IT integration took 5 years to complete. During this time customers received different levels of service depending on which bank they originally used. More recently, Royal Bank of Scotland said it could save £350 million in three years from IT synergies after its merger with Natwest: £180 million from cutting out duplication and £170 million from efficiency gains (Ranger 2001).

The centrality of IT to business processes and the high costs of infrastructure and operations mean that any M&A will include a significant area of risk associated with IT. Trends in the use of IT imply that this risk is likely to grow. In terms of the implication of this state of affairs, failure by both the merging or acquiring company and the CIO to recognise the nature and scale of IT risk inherent in their business is the first major pitfall to avoid.

The company's acquisition strategy

The second pitfall is the lack of a strategy for acquisitions on the part of the buying company. As discussed earlier there is plenty of evidence that suggests that many M&As are opportunistic, taking advantage of particular events such as a main competitor deciding to sell or a broker proposing a new opportunity. However, there is also plenty of evidence to suggest that the first thing to do right in the M&A process is to think through what needs to be achieved via acquisitions and to create criteria for selecting targets.

Box 4.2   A global goal that proved elusive

Interpublic Group (IPG) is one of the world's leaders in the marketing services sector. Early in 2000 IPG embarked on an ambitious acquisition strategy of global expansion by following their multinational clients around the world. In a period of a few years IPG acquired more than 400 new companies in the advertising world, some of them in far flung places such as Azerbaijan, Bulgaria and Kazakhstan. 'I never heard of these countries until I found that I had problems in them', joked Michael Roth, IPG's CEO.

Adopting a decentralised strategy with its new acquisitions IPG failed to integrate them. For example the IT systems of the new acquisitions were not integrated with IPG's and this decision left IPG ill-equipped to prevent inappropriate or unlawful behaviour by the employees of the new subsidiaries. The result of this 'cavalier' approach with their new acquisitions left IPG in an awkward position with the US authorities as they found difficult to reconcile some of practices in the new acquired business and their client global contracts with their obligation under US GAAP. The costs were severe in terms of financial loss. IPG reported net losses of $588 m net loss in 2004 and $139 m in the first half 2005 (IPG 2005). In professional fees alone IPG has reported a bill of $300 m in 2005 mostly for compliance with Sarbanes-Oxley. In a recent interview by the *Financial Times*, Mr Roth explained that this experience has left IPG with a few lessons to draw upon. One of them is: 'Get accounting systems in place before you go global. Interpublic's financial woes have been compounded by a failure to unify its operation's IT systems'.

Source: *Financial Times* (2005).

An M&A strategy should address the question of how often to buy and how many acquisitions are required. For instance, Bank One undertook a growth acquisition strategy from early 1970s to early 1990s whereby they would buy a company every other year to allow time to integrate and divest certain parts of the new acquisitions. This strategy allowed Bank One time to digest their new acquisitions. Other companies, however, suffered indigestion from their purchases. An example of this issue is illustrated by Interpublic Group whose voracious acquisition strategy during 2000–2004 came to haunt them after discovering that their accounting and control systems were not able to report financial results accurately in their new acquisitions (see Box 4.2).

Having an overall M&A strategy is crucial not only for the company but also for IT because a lot of the decisions that have to be made regarding system options are long term and strategic. An example of this is described in Box 4.3. At the due diligence stage for the first acquisition, it was not clear what the strategic objectives were and IT was told to spend as little as possible. The CIO adopted a tactical approach and

Box 4.3 Short-term versus long-term – the balancing act

Madrid: year 1

P2 is a well-known UK chemical company leader in its field that is looking to expand its production facilities in Europe. S2 is part of a well-known Spanish conglomerate that is looking to reduce its portfolio of non-core businesses. S2's parent company decides that S2 is not core business so it is put up for sale. S2 operates in the same business as P2 so P2 buys S2.

Shortly after the merger is announced a quick IT assessment of S2 is made by P2's CIO. This is the first European acquisition that P2 has made so there is no previous experience of how to go about integrating S2. P2 operates a decentralised business model. S2's previous parent company operated centralised operating business model and S2's IT operations were run centrally in Madrid.

A decision is made to use as much of S2's current assets as possible. Unfortunately, there is not much IT infrastructure to use because of S2's previously centralised IT operations. A decision is made to install new software packages and let S2 manage its own project. Because S2 has no IT resources of its own the whole project is outsourced to the software supplier who in turn subcontracts the implementation of the project to a small 'boutique' local software company.

It is not long before P2's CIO starts regretting his decision. The integration project is not going well. The project is running 6 months behind the original schedule and the CIO discovers that the small boutique software company is using S2's project as a bargaining tool to get paid previous amounts that the software supplier owes them. P2's CIO's Spanish is not up to coping with local Southern Spanish business rules. He thought he had chosen the right local manager (the Finance Director) to run this project but being a finance man he is not paying until he is satisfied that the boutique software company is delivering the project milestones. They in turn are waiting for the software supplier to pay them and in the meantime are working on other clients to earn some revenue and keep the company viable. P2's CIO realises that he needs external help.

An international Spanish manager is recruited in London and sent to manage the project. The new Project Manager soon gets to the bottom of all the issues, speaks the right language, introduces the right project management discipline and works with all parties involved to resolve the issues. Six months later the integration project is delivered.

Two years later: Milan

P2's European expansion continues. P2 decides to buy another S2 company this time in Italy. The similarities with the previous Spanish acquisition are striking. The Italian parent company is also a well-known chemical group. As in the previous Spanish case P2 lets the local management run the project but this time gives them the same consultant that managed the Spanish acquisition. He also applies his linguistic knowledge and project management skills to reduce the project risks and deliver the results. Unfortunately because of P2's decentralised philosophy, synergies between the new S2 and P2 are minimal.

Continued

Two years later: London

P2's position in the market is changing. The business cycle is entering a down-turn. Demand is dropping for P2's products because of competition and economic recession. P2 is under pressure to reduce costs. A new CEO is appointed and he initiates a strategic review. IT is under pressure because group management feels that IT is not providing them with adequate information systems to manage an international group which has now expanded to 50 countries and has 7 manufacturing plants in all 5 continents. They are also complaining that the decentralised IT strategy is only producing incompatible systems that do not talk to each other and that the costs of IT are too high.

P2's CIO is under pressure again, this time to consolidate and centralise.

Box 4.4   Knowing what to buy

A large US company was looking for diversification and decided to buy another US company. The acquiring company was very successful in its own oil exploration and instrument logging field. The acquired company was one of the founders of Silicon Valley and credited to be one of the pioneers in the semiconductor industry. When the acquirer company announced the deal everyone thought it was a good idea. However, what happened two years later indicated that the acquirer had bitten more than it could chew. The deal was not a success for a number of reasons and the fact that the acquirer did not have any previous experience of acquiring a large company in an entirely different industry was certainly one of them.

---

solved the short-term problem by leaving the systems at the acquired company alone instead of adopting the acquirer's. When a few years later after a further European acquisition the parent company realised that it could not manage the subsidiaries, the main reason was the inadequacy of the subsidiaries' old IT systems. At that point the IT Director was told to change the subsidiaries' systems. The system bill presented as a result of this decision amounted to several million pounds sterling, three times more than what it would have cost to change the systems during the acquisition. As a result of not having an acquisitions strategy the IT costs of acquisition outweighed the synergies.

Some mergers and acquisition strategies are higher risk than others. The larger and faster the growth envisaged in general the higher the risks. Strategies that involve diversification or internationalisation may also carry higher risks where the company is operating outside its normal area of understanding. Box 4.4 illustrates the problems that can arise where the company has adopted such a high risk strategy. In this case the IT integration was difficult and synergies were hard to realise because of the problems besetting the deal as a whole.

Box 4.5   Clear M&A criteria

In the early 1990's Tyco set out on acquisitions-driven growth strategy within four business segments: Electronics, Healthcare, Security and Flow Control. The company set four acquisition criteria: a target must be in one of these sectors; must expand product lines or improve distribution; must offer excellent growth prospects; and must use familiar technology.

Source: Mitchell and Capron 2003.

The M&A target

Identifying and selecting the target that fits the M&A strategy represents a challenge for companies. Choosing the target carefully is always important but can be vital when the company's M&A strategy is to diversify, internationalise or move into new territory. Companies that take their time in doing this get rewarded either because they find what they are looking for or if do not, they walk away from deals that might later have proved disastrous. An example of a systematic approach which builds on a mergers and acquisition strategy is given in Box 4.5.

This approach to targeting attempts to reduce the IT risks and maximise opportunities by looking for companies that use familiar business processes and technology. From a CIO view point it is important that his/her board understands the IT implications in prospective targets. For example, buying a company using the same ERP or technology platforms as the parent company will reduce the IT integration costs and risks.

The M&A decision

In M&As the deal itself defines the risks attached to the transaction. In particular this refers to the price and the terms of the M&A when set against the estimates that are made of savings and growth. The decision to buy a company is a complex business and involves multiple factors. As noted above, companies may fail to make a quality decision because of lack of strategic fit, picking the wrong company, or going into the wrong industry. However, the most important contributor to whether or not an M&A is ultimately considered to be a success is the cost–price equation.

IT can constitute a major element of both the costs and the synergies in an M&A. This is illustrated in Box 4.6 with respect to the utility sector:

This example raises the issue of the need for IT to be involved in the discussions that shape the deal.

> *Box 4.6*   IT getting involved at the very beginning
>
> In the energy supply business IT systems are very important. IT savings typically represent 25–30% of M&A synergies, along with procurement savings and these allow the economies of scale in the business operations to be achieved. On the other hand, the IT costs can amount to 50% of the total M&A integration project costs. Therefore, it is not surprising that the IT function needs to be involved at the very beginning of the M&A process.
>
> *Source*: Energy business CIO's comments.

> *Box 4.7*   IT estimates proved wrong
>
> At the time of the merger of JP Morgan Chase the bank top management said: 'We believe this merger will create pre-tax synergies of $3 bn, $2 bn of cost savings and $1 bn of incremental net revenue' Most of the synergies would materialise in two years, company officials said. A significant share of the savings would come from a consolidation and integration of information systems. After the merger the combined banks both had lower revenues and much lower profits. The main reason for this being that the IT integration effort had been grossly underestimated.
>
> *Source*: Strassmann 2003.

Whether IT is involved or not typically depends on whether IT is central to the business, or it has a particular contribution to make to the M&A decision. The latter could also be because of a particular technology used by the targeted company, a particular business skill that the CIO may have or just simply because the CEO thinks that IT should be involved. However, despite the many pointers to the relevance of IT considerations to the M&A decision, IT is not regularly involved. According to a survey by the Bathwick group (Ranger 2001) half of IT directors are not consulted before a merger happens. Fewer than half of those in companies which had undergone mergers in the last two years were asked about IT implications of the deal. A paper by Samuels (2001) reported a survey that showed that typically CEOs only involve IT heads at the latter stages of the process. 'If they are lucky, they get involved in due diligence but there are cases where IT directors are not involved and hear the announcement in the press, along with everyone else.' Failure to quantify the costs and synergies associated with an M&A accurately at the point where the deal is being made can lead to shareholders asking some very tough questions when the transaction fails to deliver promised benefits. Box 4.7 illustrates the impact that poor estimates of

IT costs can have on an M&A. The risks of getting the figures wrong are clearly greater if those with the detailed knowledge of IT, in particular the CIO, are not involved in the M&A decision.

IT strategy within the business

Strategy seems to come in cycles like fashion. When there is an economic downturn strategy becomes unfashionable because most companies have a single basic objective: survival. This is, of course, a strategy but it is only short term. In our terminology we mean strategy with a long-term horizon. Conversely, when the good times return companies start thinking of expanding and then strategy becomes fashionable again. The importance of long-term thinking is illustrated by the problems that short-term thinking implies for IT. IT deliverable cycles are being shortened all the time, but IT strategic thinking needs to have a time horizon of at least three years. Furthermore IT M&A projects are strategic and their implications are clearly several years later as shown in examples such as Box 4.3. Lack of a clear IT strategy, articulated with the business strategy, increases the risks associated with IT in an M&A.

One of the first business questions for the CIO contemplating an M&A project to ask is: does the company have a long-term business strategy? The second question is: does the business have an IT strategy? The third question is: are the two aligned? The discussion with CIOs shed some interesting light on this. All answered yes to the first two questions but the answer to the third question was less clear. In the cases based on the author's experience the answer was yes to the first question, but the answer was mixed in the relation to the second and third questions.

The importance of having three affirmatives to these questions lies in the fact that the decisions the CIO has to make with respect to IT integration need to be informed by a set of coherent strategies. Having such strategies reduces the risks associated with IT in the M&A context. Conversely, the lack of an IT strategy linked to the business strategy increases the risk that IT will be unable to achieve savings and synergies, and that it will be less able to sustain growth in business operations after the merger is completed.

Box 4.8 illustrates the problems of a company operating in the engineering sector without a clear business strategy. The second example relates to a company in the retail sector. This company made several foreign acquisitions over a four-year period but failed to achieve IT synergies because it did not have a group IT strategy. See Box 4.9.

Box 4.8   Unclear business strategy

This international company operates in the engineering field making complex machinery for the tobacco industry. In 2003 due to the ills of the tobacco industry the company needed to restructure and wanted to diversify into other related products and services. With this objective it made a foreign acquisition in Europe. Unfortunately the company's business strategy was not articulated so when the acquisition took place no IT synergies were achieved even though the size of the acquired company fitted within the parent company's existing IT systems and infrastructure. There was no IT involvement in the acquisition either. The lack of a clear business strategy was one of the key reasons for the acquisition failing to achieve its financial targets.

Box 4.9   No IT strategy, no IT synergies

This international group of companies operates in the retail sector. In 2001 the group reached market saturation on its own domestic market and decided to expand overseas. Following a successful first acquisition in Scandinavia they made others in Spain, Italy and Greece. In each case IT was involved with the due diligence but achieving IT synergies was not possible because the group lacked an overall international IT strategy.

When we made the first acquisition we did not think it was worth the trouble of integrating them with us because of different size, culture, etc. But now having made three more acquisitions we do have an urgent requirement for an overall IT strategy. The international business accounts now for 30% of our group turnover and these foreign companies are growing and our corporate systems need reviewing, so we do need a corporate IT strategy. If only my CEO could have given me the international mandate earlier.

Source: Retail business CIO's comments.

As the above examples illustrate the absence of clear business and IT strategies makes decisions on technology, people and business processes much more difficult during the post-integration stage. Often companies realise these problems too late in the M&A project mainly because IT is being thought of in tactical rather than in strategic terms. The CIO can reduce the risks associated with a possible future M&A by having in place a clear IT strategy that fits within the overall business strategy. The existence and quality of the latter may be out of the CIO's hands, but the former is firmly in the remit of the CIO.

The role of IT in the M&A team

The fundamental role of IT in the M&A team is that of support and risk management. As we have seen in the previous pages the IT risks associated with a M&A project are to do with technology assumptions in terms of IT synergies, IT costs, timescales and operational continuity. Many of these risks are created by decision making that occurs at the beginning of the M&A process at a stage where IT involvement is often limited or non-existent.

If the M&A team includes IT from the beginning of the process these risks are better assessed, quantified and planned for. A typical mistake made in the early stages without IT involvement is to make assumptions about costs savings in the IT area. The ball-park figures that financial assessors make on behalf of IT are notoriously inaccurate but once committed these figures become official and they appear in external communications. Later when IT gets involved these figures are either unachievable or if they are achievable are in exchange for taking higher IT risks.

The role of IT is invaluable to the mergers and acquisition team in more than just technical issues. If the CIO is an experienced one, his or her prior M&A experience will be very useful to the rest of the team. This experience may also be international which for international mergers would be a great asset. Another area where IT contribution is often underestimated is in the change management process. CIOs as heads of IT often have considerable experience in the implementation of change, through the introduction of new technology, business process re-engineering or outsourcing.

Most M&As involve a degree of change in the business operating model. IT is probably one of the best equipped functions in a company with the overall knowledge of the whole operation at a considerable level of detail. This is an invaluable help for the M&A director to have before making some of the decisions involving major restructuring or closure of some of the newly acquired operations.

However, it is in the area of operational risk where IT makes probably its greatest contribution. In one recent consulting assignment one of the authors was asked to help a client with their Spanish acquisition. The client wanted an assessment of the new company's systems to cope with the Christmas peak. He also wanted to know if the new company's systems could support the expected annual growth in sales. The operational risks to the business were too great without having the IT technical assessment. In this case the client took the necessary steps to involve IT right at the start of the acquisition process. Involving IT too late in the decision-making process is one of the pitfalls that should be avoided.

Due diligence

In Chapter 8 tasks involved in due diligence phase will be looked at in detail. The point to be considered in the business context is the importance of, wherever possible, undertaking the due diligence phase. On the one hand legislative pressures and the need for good information in shaping a deal emphasise the need for due diligence to be carried out. Against this, speed and secrecy, particularly in the case of a hostile or contested bid, makes due diligence difficult to accomplish. As a result, companies do not always carry out an IT due diligence. Most of the companies involved in the cases reported in the book carried one out after the merger had been announced: only two of the cases discussed did it before deciding to proceed with the merger.

Involving IT in the due diligence process is one of the best ways of reducing the IT risks in an M&A. By gathering the information outlined in Chapter 8 not only can the CIO plan the eventual integration much better but he or she can also advise the company better on the likely costs and benefits of integration that should be taken into account in making the deal. An example of the key lessons to be learned from companies that have not undertaken due diligence and identified some of the implementation issues and risks is to be found in Box 4.10.

Problems can also arise if IT due diligence is done in a hurry without allowing enough time to investigate properly. The case of C16 illustrates the difference between two acquisitions, one where due diligence was done in a hurry and the second where a combination of previous experience and better due diligence created greater synergies (see Box 4.11).

IT due diligence looks simple enough but it is not. It is an area where without previous experience is easy to miss important costs aspects as illustrated in case C15 (see Box 4.12).

Box 4.10   Driving IT integration without a roadmap

C3 approached its European merger without carrying out an IT due diligence before starting the integration project. With that benefit it could have anticipated the integration issues ahead. For example, an assessment of the selected site for the first ERP implementation would have indicated the implementation issues to do with cultural differences, skills deficiencies in the business and IT areas, the disparity of technology infrastructure, and the lack of fit between ERP functionality and business requirements. More importantly the lack of an adequate implementation team, poor project management and an overall implementation plan were things that an IT due diligence would have identified. The costs of an initial failed attempt resulted in loss of people, credibility amongst senior management of both companies and considerable delay in the completion of the project.

Source: Engineering business CIO's comments.

Box 4.11 Do not rush IT due diligence

IT was not involved prior to the announcement of the Italian acquisition. Some IT due diligence was carried out and but there was little notice given to the IT department before it was asked to get involved with the post acquisition strategy.

The German acquisition went much more smoothly than the Italian one. Among other things, previous experience helped, because at due diligence stage a good understanding was gained of what needed to be done to integrate the two companies.

Source: IT Manager's comments.

Box 4.12 Underestimating the IT integration costs in due diligence

S15 is a small independent and successful publisher operating in Europe, USA and Asia. P15 is the business-to-business division of a world leader in the publishing industry.

From an IT standpoint a due diligence is carried out by P15's own internal IT management. Soon after the acquisition is completed a new IT Director is recruited. His role is to implement the IT integration strategy. The integration strategy has 3 basic objectives:

1. address all short-term issues identified in the due diligence,
2. move IT infrastructure to Microsoft platform, and
3. carry out an orderly change in the IT organisation.

The overall IT approach is to move gradually towards a P15 IT model without destroying some of the strong IT features inherent in S15's operating model in the process. However, soon after taking over, the new IT Director realised that S15's IT infrastructure was falling short in terms of capacity and resilience and some of the systems suffered from repeated lack of investment. He also identified further risks which required a higher and more urgent investment than those identified in the IT due diligence.

The combination of S15's high IT operating costs (running about 10% of sales at the time of the acquisition and 5% higher than industry standard) and also the requirement for higher capital expenditure than originally expected made the IT contribution less significant than it could have been. According to the IT Director 'the decision to buy S15 was made on the strength of S15's current and future profitability and IT involvement came much later on in the acquisition process. To be honest no IT synergies were assumed at the time of making the purchase but it also meant that the cost of updating IT systems was underestimated in my view'.

Source: Media business CIO's comments.

The message is that IT due diligence is one of the best ways to reduce the IT risks in an M&A. It should therefore be done thoroughly and be allocated sufficient time and expertise to ensure that risks are recognised and documented as fully as possible.

The implementation timetable

The nature and high profile of the M&A integration project often sets unrealistic deadlines. Normally the dates are fixed and cannot be changed without creating bad publicity that can be used by the media and can have an impact on the financial position of the parent company. From a financial viewpoint time costs money and speed of execution is important. However, setting deadlines for IT without understanding the implications makes the achievement of IT post-integration synergies doubtful and later puts the CIO onto the back foot. This is hardly the right approach to achieve IT synergies and success.

Two examples from our research show this. In the first example the parent company rushed through the integration without considering the people and soft systems issues thus losing key staff and failing to achieve the synergies expected (see Box 4.13). In the second case aggressive deadlines and poor planning made the initial ERP implementation fail and put the post-merger IT integration at risk (see Box 4.14).

Box 4.13   Speed is not always best

C8 is one of the leading international companies in the area of water treatment programs. In 2002 after a previous failed merged with another company C8 was sold to P8. P8 is a well known international industrial conglomerate.

The acquisition approach taken by P8 was geared to quick execution of integration activities with the emphasis placed on speed. Based on previous acquisitions P8 had an IT plan from the start and proceeded to implement it applying the 80/20 rule rather than aiming to get 100% right. The process was executed ruthlessly with most of the European IT infrastructure being outsourced to places like India, Spain and USA.

One of the lessons from this acquisition was that fast execution is not always the best. For example some valuable people were lost too quickly and that created its own set of problems including delay (and hence cost) in achieving some of the integration targets including some customer interface programs.

Source: Engineering business CIO's comments.

Box 4.14 Unrealistic implementation deadlines

P3 is very successful; an acquisitive company operating in the process control and engineering field. Although P3 had a well-tested and successful methodology for buying companies and getting synergies out of them in financial terms, their international IT expertise was limited at the time. From their US IT Centre in Minneapolis they despatched a small task force with the view of rolling out their chosen ERP system in Europe. Without any previous international experience in their IT team and no formal IT due diligence of their newly acquired European sites they soon started hitting major problems. It was at this point they decided to get a new CIO.

Source: Engineering business CIO's comments.

Box 4.15 Customers can be hurt

In my first M&A experience working as IT Manager the parent company (a large US multinational company in the semi-conductor industry) rushed the implementation of new systems following its acquisition with disastrous consequences. Because the parent company insisted on discontinuing the acquired company systems and moving to a new untested system, the fall-out that followed the system changeover meant goods going to the wrong customers, invoices sent with wrong addresses, customer orders being lost, etc. The result was a loss of customer and employee confidence with the resulting losses in customers employees and corporate reputation. The IT issues were a contributory reason for this acquisition failing to achieve their pre-merger objectives.

Source: Manufacturing business CIO's comments.

Most CEOs do not appreciate the complexities and effort required to integrate IT systems after a merger. For example, in a merger it is common to come across different systems that use different data structures and architectures. In order to exchange data between the two systems detailed analysis, design and conversion of the existing applications are required. These tasks when undertaken in a hurry (typically the integration of critical systems after a merger is expected in less than 3 months) are prone to error and increase the costs and delay the benefits of a merger. The costs of rushing can be very high as illustrated in Box 4.15.

Many CEOs are either not interested in or are unable to grasp IT complexities when considering a merger and they accept quite readily IT costs-saving estimates that are reliant on unrealistic rule of thumb multipliers. These hastily taken assumptions add to the risks of overestimating the IT benefits from a merger and by default increase the pressure put on IT to deliver to 'unrealistic time scales'.

Management of the M&A process

Chapter 6 discusses the crucial role that the CIO plays in managing risk through his or her management of the integration process. However the CIO's leadership and management role takes place within the context provided by the wider management of the merger within the company. Companies approach managing the process in different ways: some approaches contain and reduce risk better than others. For example, some companies will be driven by a strong leader; others will pay more importance to the speed and results. Some will have a detailed process, others will do very little planning. Some will be more people-centric, others will be less so. IT as part of the M&A process will be affected by these differences.

The cultural setting of the acquired company, and the approach that the parent company takes to it, determines the pace of change. IT will need to adjust their method appropriately. A clash of cultures between two companies can impose constraints in IT in terms of additional requirements that make the implementation of the integration project more difficult. The management of a cross-border acquisition can be particularly demanding both for the company as a whole and for the IT function. This is illustrated in the case presented in Box 4.16 where additional time had to be given to satisfy Swedish requirements before they could adopt the parent company's system.

Culture can also determine a particular technology or organisational model. In the case of C6 the parent company insisted that all new acquisitions adopted the parent's own business model and centralised IT system. That enabled IT to get the new company up and running virtually within days. Such an outcome was only possible as a result of strong leadership and clearly directed management of the acquisition by the acquiring company.

Box 4.16   Planning for incompatible cultures pays off

Stockholm

P4 is a medium-size US manufacturing multinational company. Bought two years previously by an American venture capital group for investment purposes P4's owners are interested in a fast expansion programme to build P4's future earning potential. S4 is a manufacturing division of a well-known Swedish company operating in the mobile communications business. The acquisition rationale for P4 is to keep S4's parent as one of its key customers and expand its international operations in Sweden. The selling objectives for S4's parent are to off load its manufacturing costs and securing its source of supply by a long-term contract with P4.

Continued

P4 operates a regional IT model with each world region USA, Europe and Asia-Pacific running autonomously. In Europe all operations are centralised in Holland and a standard ERP system supports all the manufacturing sites in France, Ireland and Holland. S4 runs all its IT operations from a central hub located in the parent's company in Stockholm.

The technology and systems infrastructure are different and there are very few points of IT synergy between the two companies.

Before the merger is made public, P4 develops a detailed acquisition plan that includes IT and contains a reasonably accurate assessment of S4's IT organisation, systems and infrastructure.

As soon as the merger is made public P4's integration team is put to work. The integration team has been carefully selected and contains members from both P4 and S4 and external consultants in specific areas including IT. To cope with the cultural differences the team includes multi-lingual members who speak English, Dutch, German and Swedish and are internationally experienced having worked in foreign countries before.

The IT joint team has an integration plan within days. This task is simplified by the decision taken at the onset that S4's current systems will be discontinued and S4 will use P4 systems instead. The main technical difficulties revolve around S4 data to feed P4 systems and P4 systems to meet S4 business requirements. The data requirements are time consuming but resolved successfully. The problem of P4's functionality is more serious.

When S4 requirements are investigated closely it is discovered that the problem is to do with S4's business processes, which are based on the way that S4 operates, which in turn is based on Swedish logic with a distinctly strong cultural content. In other words to understand the problem and to find an acceptable solution one needs to understand the Swedish way of thinking. This issue soon becomes critical.

A process for dealing with this issue is agreed that allows enough time and participation for the Swedish members to agree a solution which is accepted them. It is here where the international experience and multi-lingual capabilities of the integration team, in particular the Dutch members, win the day. Had the situation had to be resolved by the American or the Swedish members alone, coming from such different cultures the task would have been much more difficult.

In the end a suitable pragmatic compromise is made possible by all sides giving something away and getting something back. For example, P4's system's functionality is enhanced by making some immediate changes that accommodated some of S4's more urgent requirements, with others to be made later. In return S4 drops some of its own requirements, agreeing to adopt P4's businesses processes instead. To help with these changes personnel from P4 and S4 agreed to work in each others' countries and learn about each others' practices.

The integration project took 6 months to complete in line with the plan agreed at the beginning of the project.

In order to reduce the risks associated with IT in an M&A the management of the overall processes within the company and within the IT function must be aligned. The acquiring company needs to appreciate the management problems encountered by IT and the IT integration needs to be managed within the culture and management expectations of the company as a whole. Especially where a complex, cross-border acquisition is involved this calls for some give and take.

Prior mergers and acquisition experience

Avoiding the many pitfalls of an M&A is easier if the company, and the CIO, have been involved in an M&A project before (see Box 4.17). The CIOs who took part in the discussion saw previous mergers and acquisition experience as highly significant for the ability of IT to make a substantial contribution to the success of the transaction. Samuels (2001) states that 'CIOs who have not been through this process before end up making big decisions on little information'. He concludes, further, that in these circumstances it is difficult for the CIO to create value from a newly merged company. Increased M&A activity is likely to increase the number of CIOs with relevant experience. However the knowledge gap is likely to remain, and in order that it does not become a risk factor, it must be filled as far as possible by drawing on knowledge located elsewhere or outside the department.

Box 4.17   Loaning from experience

When P1 and S1 merged in most people thought that the merger would be very successful. Unfortunately P1 did not consider it important to involve IT until after the announcement had been made. The fact that the merger was not seen as friendly one by one of the sides perhaps had something to do with it. However, the costs of late IT involvement were too high. Two and a half years after the merger had been announced the two companies had not managed to implement IT systems that worked. Lack of IT involvement, poor planning and aggressive and unrealistic deadlines made IT one of the culprits for the merger failing to achieve its M&A targets. The reality was, however, that no one in the acquiring senior management understood the importance of IT in helping to pull off the merger. The consequences of loss of business, loss of people and confidence in the enlarged group as a result of the IT fallout could have been avoided by getting IT involved right at the beginning. The moral of the story is that the same company has learned the lessons and today their IT is central to their business.

Source: Senior Manager's comments (a few years after the merger).

The same issue arises at the corporate level. In this case although the CIO may have experience that is relevant to an M&A, the company or organisation within which he or she works may not. When it comes to an international M&A the prior experience is even more important. For example, in the case presented in Box 4.16. the assembling of an experienced and multilingual IT team made a significant difference in the way the newly acquired Swedish company's IT requirements were met.

In a study by John Child *et al.* (2003) a strong correlation was found between previous international M&A experience by the parent company and success in integration and profitability after the merger. Experience provides confidence in the management team and the combination of the two is a strong recipe for success. One of the implications for IT is that, if the acquiring company is uncertain about what to do with the new acquisition, it will be happy to get a certain level of information about the target and leave the acquired company to carry on with their own systems. In our experience this approach causes several problems for IT because:

1. Few or no IT synergies are achieved
2. Integration problems with the parent company create inefficiencies later on
3. When integration is required (typically 2 or 3 years later) the IT integration costs are much higher.

5
Technical Issues

Incompatible technology is one the most common factors that increases the IT risks in an M&A project because it increases the integration costs. Reducing this risk may involve selecting common single-technology architecture and associated technical solutions. One of the advantages of the single-technology approach will be increased economies of scale. The main disadvantages will be the time required to gain support, resistance to change and delayed implementation. Untested technology is another common IT pitfall in an M&A project and companies that take this approach increase their IT risks. It should be minimised as much as possible. Data migration, system interfaces and scalability are typically underestimated when it comes to meeting agreed timescales and costs.

Our research supports the view that in order to manage these IT issues successfully the CIO must have a clear IT technical strategy and vision when contemplating an M&A integration project. For example, is there a standard policy regarding technology? Are standard packages to be used as part of this policy? Is a centralised IT model to be pursued or should flexibility be allowed in the post-acquisition system integration? All these decisions should be clear in the CIO's mind before entering the post-integration activities. Managing the IT issues themselves is fundamental for reducing M&A IT risks and spotting opportunities. Failing to resolve the technical issues successfully will not do the CIO's career any good and may also put the whole M&A project in peril.

The top 10 technical issues that arise during an M&A project that were identified during the interviews are shown in Box 5.1 These are all issues that need to be identified as early as possible in the M&A process although their impact may not be fully felt until the integration project is underway. These issues fall into two groups:

1. Issues related to the technology involved in the M&A transaction.
2. Issues related to the IT strategy adopted that have technical implications.

Box 5.1 Top 10 IT issues

1. Incompatible technology
2. Untested technology
3. Interface problems
4. Scalability
5. Data migration
6. Lack of standard systems
7. In-sourcing versus outsourcing
8. Centralised versus decentralised systems
9. In-house versus packages
10. Small versus big company

Technology

Incompatible technology

Incompatible technology is to a greater or lesser extent an IT issue in most mergers and it is frequently underestimated during the preliminary M&A negotiations. Even companies operating in the same industry come across incompatible IT technology. With the advent of open standards and the internet this is becoming less of an issue, but it still represents a substantial part of the IT work and IT costs during the merging process because of the number of old (legacy) systems still around. In some industries such as banking and retailing it is not unusual to find back office systems 20 years old.

Incompatible systems are also found in companies that use the same technology. For example, it is common to see companies supporting multiple versions of the same operating systems. In a recent assignment that one of the authors was involved in the client organisation had four different versions of Windows operating system, three versions of Unix and three versions of Oracle database. The maintenance effort and costs of supporting all these disparate systems was substantial, let alone the costs and effort of integrating them in another company.

There is certainly evidence in our research that points to this issue being encountered by a number of the CIOs. An example from C16 illustrates the case where the CIO faced two mergers with incompatible technology (see Box 5.2). Similarly, in the case of C3 the incompatible technology in this merger set back the integration schedule by several months (see Box 5.3). These two cited cases involved very large companies where this issue is generally very complex but incompatible technology affects companies of all sizes.

Box 5.2   Incompatible technology: example 1

C16 is the European operation of a main division of a well-known global oil company operating in 145 countries and employing over 115,000 employees worldwide. C16 processes crude oil into refineries and markets innovative products to 25,000 customers worldwide. Over its famous history it has grown through a combination of organic growth, joint ventures and acquisitions.

In the last 7 years C16 has been involved in two European acquisitions, the first one in Italy in 1997 and the second one in Germany in 2002. Both acquisitions were the result of joint ventures between C16's country subsidiaries and local companies operating in the same business.

The contribution expected from IT was to reduce IT operating costs and technical complexity and establish economies of scale wherever possible by using, for example, C16's existing European IT data centre infrastructure in Holland. The process to achieve these objectives was complicated.

Secondly, the IT technology platforms used in each company were different (e.g. IBM main frame versus AS 4000; Ethernet versus token ring).

Thirdly, the culture of the two IT organisations was also different, one being used to design and develop new systems in house, the other used to employ standard packages.

The result of this incompatibility translated into considerably more time and effort to resolve them than originally envisaged.

Source: Extracts from CIO's interview.

Incompatible technology complicates the IT integration work because it requires the IT staff's technical skills from both companies increasing the M&A risks and the retention of such skills may in itself be difficult. As a result of the different technology deployed the technical communications are often difficult. Technical IT staff are not always the easiest people to communicate with and the question of which technical language to use is not only a technical issue but also a cultural one too.

In one large merger in which one of the authors worked, the parent and subsidiary used completely different hardware and software systems. The communications between the two IT organisations resembled two people talking different languages despite the fact English was the local language for both of them. The CIO had to recruit 'translators' who had worked in both technical environments before so they could design the appropriate conversion interfaces. As each group used different technology the process of integrating the two IT departments took more effort and was more complex than originally planned.

Box 5.3 Incompatible technology: example 2

P3 is very successful and acquisitive company operating in the process control and engineering field. S3 also operates in the same business but most of its product line is complimentary to P3 so the rationale for the merger is sound. S3 is bought by P3 and the acquisition doubles its size (P3 and S3 are of similar size and have a combined turnover of circa $3.2 Billion). Both are major manufacturing divisions of their respective parents operating in a multitude of markets worldwide.

Being an experienced international M&A operator P3 uses their experience for selecting the new management team and this is announced at the same time as the merger is made public.

The culture of P3 is assertive, very focussed on numbers and no nonsense approach. By contrast S3's culture is more of an engineering culture, paternalistic and people oriented.

Their IT systems are very different.

P3 operates a decentralised IT function with small data centres in each country and standard application packages which because of its many previous acquisitions have been implemented ad-hoc and their IT strategy has not been very successful. P3's international infrastructure is old and in need of replacement. In fact, just before the merger with S3 P3 had decided to put a standard ERP package in all its operations.

S3 operates a regional model with strategic data centres in the main areas of the world where they operate. Within Europe there are 3 regional data centres based in UK, Holland and France. S3 uses a mixture of software packages and in-house developed systems. Like P3 some of S3's systems are 10 years old and need replacing.

The result of this diversity in equipment, organisation and systems made the integration effort much harder than originally thought and set back the original integration schedule by nearly 12 months.

Source: Extracts from engineering company C3.

Suppliers of incompatible technology have to be dealt with after a merger. This adds complexity to the post-merger implementation process. For instance, in another case known to the authors, a small company was totally dependent on one supplier. When this company was acquired it adopted the new parent's system. Buying the old supplier out from existing contracts was a complex business. In the case of a merger of two large multinationals, which used incompatible technology suppliers, the negotiations involved long-term contracts that amounted to tens of millions of dollars. In addition to the financial aspects of these contracts one should also be aware of the amount of 'political positioning' that follows a merger of this type among suppliers and by internal IS staff. This also makes the integration more complex and longer than originally planned.

The message for the CIO is that he or she must plan for finding various degrees of incompatible technology in the acquired company and take this into account in his/her initial integration plan. He or she will no doubt take stock of the key differences during the due diligence face and should prepare an integration plan that deals with technical issues accordingly. The integration project may indeed present him or her with an opportunity to reduce technical complexity by adopting a single systems standard approach but for reasons of timing most CIOs will adopt a more conservative and short term approach by developing bridges among the differing technology layers by means of interfaces (see page 63 below).

Untested technology

This issue manifests itself in one of two ways. One is as the consequence of very tight deadlines that M&A IT projects suffer from. The second one is more deliberate and it is as a consequence of decisions made at the time of the acquisition.

In the first instance during an M&A the CIO may need to integrate systems that have never worked in this way before. This could be where systems are linked via interfaces or because existing systems need to do something new. The amount of time required to make these system changes frequently exceeds the amount of time allowed for the M&A project. Risks are exceptionally high in such uncharted waters: for example a small technical detail can cause a major breakdown in the business operation (see Box 5.4).

The combination of unfamiliar technology, top management expectations in terms of timescales, and IT management's lack of time to sort out problems can cause problems to spiral out of control as illustrated in Box 5.5.

Box 5.4   System changes stops all printing for 6 days!

This international company acquired a German subsidiary. During the IT integration everything worked well until the last minute. Although all the main IT activities were completed on time and worked well a small technical point involving the printing facility was overlooked and as a result printing was not possible for 6 days!

Source: Extracts from manufacturing company CIO interview.

Box 5.5   It pays off to getting IT right

New York

P1 is a very successful company in the oil business. S1 is also very successful in the semiconductor business but needs a lot of cash to fund its R&D. P1 needs S1 technology and has lots of cash. Merger is announced and everyone seems to think is a good idea.

London

9 months have passed since the merger was announced and systems integration is becoming more urgent. A task force with US and European IT managers and IT specialists is assembled. An initial plan is drawn and broad principles are agreed but a detailed system map is not available. P1 wants to replace S1 systems with standard IBM hardware which P1 uses and standard software packages which is new to P1 and S1 but it will save time and money.

Paris

After closer evaluation of European businesses' needs the standard software package is rejected on the grounds of functionality, cost of changing it and time. A decision is made that US manufacturing plants will be 'encouraged' to use this package but European sales offices will develop their own software. A decision is also made to split the development among the European countries to save time. UK will develop the order processing module, Germany will be responsible for the 'traffic' (logistics) module, France for purchasing and Italy for the quote module. Each country recruits the appropriate IS resources to carry out the work within an allocated budget.

In the meantime pressure is mounting. Merger costs are escalating and the political temperature in New York is rising. P1 CEO has given S1 General Managers (GMs) an ultimatum: 'Get your IT systems ready or get fired'. S1 GMs give the same message to the Financial Directors (FDs) who are responsible for IT. FDs are doing the same with the IT Managers. They in turn are pushing their own staff as hard as they can. No one is happy.

London/Paris/Milan/Munich

An emergency meeting is held in each country to decide whether to switch to the new systems or suffer the financial and personal consequences of being the last to switch over. P1's CIO has come up with a wise stratagem and computation whereby countries that do not switch to the new system will face heavy financial penalties. Out of the 4 countries only France says she is ready. After another emergency meeting among P1 and S1 senior management it is decided that all Europe will switch to the new system by the end of the month. The IT Managers' assessment that systems are not ready is overruled and the date for change over is fixed.

D-Day arrives and systems are switched over with parts of the system not fully tested. Everyone is working around the clock. The record is held by Germany

Continued

where their IT Manager has worked 3 days without stop. Data errors and file corruptions are occurring among the various European software modules. The log of unmatched sales order to shipments is 10 pages long after the first day of operation.

Month-end processing arrives. The situation is really desperate. Bill to Shipments control reports cannot be reconciled. Customers are complaining that they have not received their orders or have received the wrong goods. The amount of data errors is still mounting and cleansing routines are not working properly. More IS experts are called in to resolve the situation. The first management resignations begin.

Source: Extracts from engineering company C1.

Box 5.6   A case of untested technology [Box 4.14 Contd]

St Louis (Corporate Headquarters)

Although P3 has a well-tested and successful methodology for buying compa-nies and getting synergies out of them in financial terms, their international IT expertise is limited. Out of their US IT Centre in Minneapolis they despatch a small task force with the view of rolling out their new chosen ERP system in Europe. Without carrying out a formal IT due diligence of S3 European sites and without any international experience in their IT team C3's corporate squad soon start hitting major problems.

London (European HQ)

P3's attempts to roll out their ERP into S3 sites are failing. After 6 months of efforts the implementation of the new ERP package in Holland has failed. The main reasons are: 1. The ERP package had just been released in the US market. (P3 has had the package on a beta mode for 6 months effectively 'debugging it'), 2. ERP functionality is geared to the US market and cannot cope with some of the European requirements, 3. ERP supplier's support in Europe is very poor, 4. Unrealistic implementation deadlines on behalf of P3, 5. Little understanding of the European business requirements as not detailed IT due diligence done and 6. Poor people management and communications.

P3 CIO comes to Europe with only one objective in mind: 'sort it all out'.

Source: Extracts from engineering company C3.

The second situation relates to when a company, normally the parent company, decides to test new technology with a new acquisition. How the decision is made varies from case to case. Sometimes it is because the parent company wants to adopt a new standard package and prefers to let the new acquisition take the risks, on the basis that the risks will be lower. In another example that the authors know well the subsidiary needed a new system and the parent company agreed to let them have a new ERP system. In a third case the new system was agreed as a compromise solution. Whatever the reason for putting in new technology during an M&A, the CIO must be aware of the pitfalls (see Box 5.6).

New technology can be particularly difficult to implement, takes time and should be minimised as much as possible during an integration project. When it is required for good reasons it should be planned thoroughly and the risks should be properly evaluated and communicated. The worst scenario of having to undertake the implementation of new technology in a hurry without adequate protection in terms of resources and budgets should be avoided.

Interface problems

When the two companies decide to keep their own systems, wholly or partly, there is a need to exchange information between their separate systems. Each situation is dependent on the technology used. The first IT technical issue that often comes up is: who have we got that understands the legacy systems in detail in both companies? Legacy systems pose particular problems.

1. By definition legacy systems are old. If they are standard packages and have been implemented a long time ago, it is likely that they have been changed and the expertise may no longer reside in the current IT department. In certain cases it may be the end users of the particular system that may be able to help, if not in technical terms, in explaining the history of the application and how it runs from an operational point of view. If the systems to be interfaced with have been developed in-house the same problem may occur. In this case it may be more difficult to find anyone with that expertise and the CIO may have to find the technical IT developer that originally put the system in.
2. Related to the expertise issue is the question of the technology used. A lot of legacy systems, particularly in the mainframe arena, were designed a long time ago and some of the technology may no longer be supported.
3. Communications among the IT technical staff are important. If the two departments use very different technology with no common standards between the two companies the design, developing and testing of the interface programs may be difficult and take longer than expected.
4. Key staff needed to do the technical interface work are required. Even if the two IT departments are kept separate it is likely that a re-organisation may affect people's position and this may trigger the decision of people to leave. Most critical are staff that have irreplaceable knowledge of how legacy systems work.

With the arrival of web-based systems and tools the technical interface issues are becoming more manageable but this is an area that will continue to consume considerable time and technical resource and should be planned carefully. The CIO should be prepared for this issue and should make realistic estimates as to the time and effort required. If this is difficult or not possible adequate contingency planning should be undertaken. For example, the CIO should insure that technical skills required for the interface work are available internally or be prepared to pay for them in the market place. This takes additional time and cost and should never be a surprise to the M&A team half-way the integration project.

Scalability

With an increase in the size of M&As the demand for even more hardware storage is increasing. We will see later in this chapter (see Box 5.15) that a central system is particularly vulnerable to scalability problems. Luckily the advances in storage technology are allowing systems to store larger and larger amounts of information. However, this advantage itself creates other associated problems such as system performance. System performance is particularly important for front-end systems and back-bone networks because they are more noticeable and affect many more end users than back-office systems.

Companies operating in public facing mode such as banks and airlines, just to mention two, are particularly vulnerable. When the merger between Barclay's Bank and The Woolwich Building Society was first discussed in 2000 banking consultants warned that scalability was a key technical issue (see Box 5.7).

A similar situation occurred when Go and easyJet airlines merged (see Box 5.8).

Box 5.7   Bank merger – scalability flagged as an issue

'The merger between Barclays Bank and the Woolwich will stretch scalability of the Woolwich on-line banking services, consultants warned'.

The consultant raised concerned over the volume of customers that the Woolwich's on-line banking and mortgage service, One-Plan could handle. The One-Plan system had at the time 290,000 customers, compared to more than one million customers for Barclays' on-line banking system.

'One of issues has got to be scalability', said a banking industry consultant. 'The Woolwich system appears to be very robust but you are looking at a customer base of 16 million. It will have to be a very well architected system'.

Source: Huber (2004), p. 4.

Box 5.8   Airline merger – scalability a key issue

The £374 million merger between Go and easy-Jet consolidated two competitors in the market creating an airline that was double the size of the previous separate businesses and promised an even lower cost base through economies of scale.

In the IT system rationalisation process that followed the merger announcement, scalability became an issue for what to keep and what to replace according to IT Manager Blair Stewart.

'Some systems simply could not cope with the doubled volume they were expected to handle, instead of the 25% annual growth which is the norm for each airline Some vendors were confident that their systems could cope, but they could not'.

Source: Vowler (2003).

In other industries such as retail a very similar situation occurs. In a consulting assignment undertaken by one of the authors the client's new acquired company was running an old legacy system and it was uncertain whether it could cope with the expected growth. A technical sizing project was set-up to carry out stress tests on the legacy system. During the volume simulation tests it became apparent that the system would be able to cope with the expected data volumes for the first six months but that during the Christmas shopping peak its storage capacity would be exceeded. It was therefore recommended that additional new and more powerful hardware was installed in order to be able to cope with the new workloads.

Scalability is an issue that affects not only systems but also network bandwidth and IT infrastructure in general. In planning an IT integration project the CIO needs to have an overall IT strategy where economical scalability should be part of it. By economical scalability we mean elasticity in the demand for network bandwidth, computing power and storage. The post-integration IT strategy should contain large segments of IT infrastructure that should be continually available to achieve scalability and reservoirs of computing power should also be planned for and available free of charge until used.

Data migration

Although IT management is aware of the importance of data migration two out of three acquisitions underestimate the effort required to get data migration right. This can be as a result of poor planning, lack of understanding of the acquired company's systems data, lack of suitable resources to carry out the data migration activity or a combination of all three.

One of the critical activities during the data migration phase is to ensure that the merged customer databases work properly. The first 'hurdle' is to make accurate calculations about the storage requirements. Most IT departments underestimate this aspect:

> Never underestimate how much horsepower and how much data storage you will need. We ended up tripling our original estimates, mostly to support the multiple versions of converted data during the testing phases. (McDonald 2003)

The second, and perhaps more subtle issue, is to recognise that changes in technology and business process may be required as a result of data migration. For example, 'some of the data in the two systems may have profoundly different data structures and architectures which may require redesign of the application' (McDonald 2003).

Box 5.9   Data migration 1: utility company

In the energy supply business Customer Information systems (CIS) are critical. Any successful M&A must ensure that the CIS can be integrated; otherwise the M&A will not work.

From the technology point of view the main issue was data migration. When handling large amounts of data involving millions of customers the main challenge was how to complete the data migration in a single week-end adopting a big-bang approach. The quality of the data migration was critical to run its operations smoothly from day one following the cutover.

Source: Extracts from CIO's interview.

Box 5.10   Data migration 2: bank

Our biggest milestone was to convert NatWest customer data to RBS's IT platform. This was scheduled to be done over a week-end and involved thousands of conversion jobs, migrating 250GB of data and transferring 14 million customer records and 33 m direct debit records. From a planning perspective it involved 4,200 people and 9,200 milestones!

On the week-end of 4 October 2002 the process started by closing down NatWest systems, converting and migrating the data, then opening for business on the RBS platforms while ensuring that customer service such as ATMs remained available.

By the end it was an enormous success and on 7 October 2002 the data migration process ended without any disruption to customer service.

Source: Watson (2003), p. 18.

The question of transferring large volumes of data in a short space of time is also a major issue as shown in the two examples in Boxes 5.9 and 5.10.

Strategy

Lack of standard systems

There is evidence to suggest that lack of standard systems is responsible for high IT implementation costs in a post-integration project, in some cases as much as 50 per cent (Hoffman 1999). This is to do with running multiple systems that become expensive to support. Hoffman argues that 'it is only after the deal closes that it is realised that data structures are incompatible and will require more investment than originally anticipated'. He also stated that integrating different computing environments takes longer and requires up to 40 per cent more effort than standardised systems.

Other IT writers concur with this view. One way to reduce implementation and post integration costs is to have a 'single technology base' (Goodwin 1999). IT architecture based on business strategy, standards and best practices can reduce time-to-market and increase return on investment (Fournier 1999). Our own research confirms some of these points. By using standard systems C6 achieved very quick integration and economies of scale in IT operations, maintenance and purchasing (see Box 5.11).

A lack of standard systems and systems standards makes M&A IT integration work difficult. This situation arises more often when the parent company does not have a clear IT strategy with its own standard systems; or when it is felt that the subsidiary's own systems cannot or should not be changed for example because they are better than the parent's own systems. In such cases they need to co-exist. In a company that one of the authors knows well the parent company had to leave the acquired company with their own systems because the parent company had no standard systems. In a separate assessment of the IT function in the parent company after the acquisition it was discovered that the parent company operated a very complex technical environment with 8 different operating systems, 85 different software products and multiple hardware platforms. In this situation it is clear why the parent company's senior management decided to leave the acquired company IT systems alone.

A lack of standards also complicates the integration not only in the technical sense but in the political one too. In this situation subsidiaries may be very reluctant to give up their technology. This in turn prevents other structural changes such in relation to people and business processes

---

Box 5.11   Standardisation brings benefits

C6 is one of the largest suppliers of timber and building materials in the United Kingdom. Since 1988 when C6 was created as a result of the merger of two separate groups the company has been growing steadily from a combination of organic growth and acquisition. Today the group consists of more than 700 branches covering the UK market. The group had a turnover of £1.6 bn in 2003.

Since 1988 C6 has experienced nearly 100 separate acquisitions and has developed a standard approach to IT systems integration following an acquisition. The standard model is based on mature systems continuously enhanced with technical innovations which have served C6 well since 1992. For example, using EDI links C6 insures up-to-date information and service to its customers and suppliers.

The standard integration model runs on a centralised super HP computer which supports 6,500 users in over 700 branches. The beauty of this centralised model says C6's CIO is that 'enables us to get a new acquisition up and running typically in 24 hours after the acquisition has been announced'.

Other advantages of the centralised system according to the CIO are: a standard set of procedures which cut down on the learning curve and offer C6's management a consistent view of the performance of the new business, low IT support and maintenance costs and a very efficient IT operation though economies of scale. On the downside there have been scaling and system performance problems that fortunately have been overcome through recent technology advances in computer power.

Source: CIO's interview comments.

---

taking place during the integration project. Implementing standard systems simplifies the decision-making process and to a large extent the implementation process too, but it is not easy if the subsidiary has had a previous culture of autonomy and decentralisation and disagrees with the approach. For the new standards to stick it is essential that they meet the subsidiary's business requirements and are supported by the senior management of the combined group.

The message for the CIO is to develop a clear set of industry standards that can be implemented anywhere in the world. The standards should cover software, hardware and communications technology. By choosing industry standards based on Unix or *de-facto* standards based on Microsoft or SAP the integration risks will be reduced at least from a technology view point.

In-sourcing versus out-sourcing

The trend to outsource IT services has been growing in recent years in response to a number of external factors such as the 'millennium bug', escalating IT costs and hard economic times. There are, however, signs that the 'insourcing trend is bringing it all back home' (Samuels 2005). According to consultants Deloitte nearly two-thirds of organisations have already brought back in-house some of their previously outsourced IT services (Samuels 2005).

In the M&A context this issue manifests itself in one of two ways:

1. As a result of a particular M&A transaction where one of the parties is tied to an outsourcing deal.
2. As a result of a strategic decision to outsource or insource at the time of the integration project.

In the first case the CIO will need to consider the pros and cons of continuing with the outsource contract, renegotiating it or terminating it. Commercial aspects will be a key consideration for the CIO in terms of costs, quality, service provision, contract duration and type of supplier. From a technology view point the ability to control the technology to respond quickly to the business needs and the provision by the supplier of the right technical skills will be major considerations for the CIO. In situations where there is no flexibility in the contract or the costs of achieving a better deal are too high the CIO may need to renegotiate or re-think the outsourcing deal.

The decision to bring the outsourced IT services back in house is a complex one and must be carefully evaluated because of the many factors involved as illustrated in Box 5.12. Apart from the financial aspects in terms of costs and benefits; the recruitment of new IT staff with appropriate technical skills; legal work contracts and organisational change are major points for the CIO to ponder. Other key considerations such as time and executive management support will make the CIO's decision even more difficult. This option is certainly not one to make in a hurry, yet sometimes this is precisely what the CIO will actually face. In that situation it helps if there is a clear IT strategy and previous experience of bringing IT services back in-house.

In the second case the CIO may for expediency, business and/or operational reasons decide to outsource the newly acquired company IT department. If this is the case he or she should be aware of the many pitfalls associated with outsourcing contracts. Choosing the right combination of suppliers ('do not put all the eggs in one basket'), a clear contract with review and get-out clauses, retaining control for key technology decisions and allowing changes and flexibility are some of the by-words for the CIO to pay attention to. According to Gartner eight in every ten organisations attempt to renegotiate their supplier

Box 5.12   Insourcing brings IT efficiencies at a major Telco company

In 1998 Cable & Wireless (C&W) entered into a 10-year, £1.8 bn outsourcing deal with IBM for the latter to run its IT infrastructure and customer billing systems. Half way through its duration C&W started its transition to bring the systems and infrastructure back in-house in order to regain control of its IT systems and technology.

According to CIO, Martin Taylor, one of the reasons was 'to be able to change our systems in order to respond to the business through a period of rapid change. But the changes did not come quickly or easy'. Looking back, Taylor said: 'insourcing was a complex process taking several months and it is one of the most difficult projects I have been through at the company'. Much of the complexity was to do with regulation governing the transfer of undertakings: protection of employment (TUPE), technolgy transfer and change management.

By insourcing its IT operations C&W has achieved benefits in efficiency ('service first not costs', says Taylor). Total costs and cost of ownerhsip have come down dramatically, at C&W, according to benchmarking database company Compass. The key lessons from the C&W experience are:

– look at the business in discrete chunks
– maintain transparency and executive control
– make sure that everything is in order before you outsource
– do not outsource a problem, outsource a system

Source: Samuels (2005).

outsourcing contracts before the deal expires. This is because normally companies are 'lax when it comes to contract writing and the all-important benchmarking for service provision' (Samuels 2005)

The choice of whether to insource or outsource is much more complicated in a merger than in an acquisition. As the example of the merger between JP Morgan Chase & Co. and Bank One Corp. illustrates the strategic IT choices get mixed with different cultures and personalities providing a challenge for the winning CIO (see Box 5.13).

From a technology perspective it is important that the CIO retains control of the IT architecture and does not outsource strategic decisions such as the choice of systems and technology platforms and that the technical skills required to manage the suppliers are retained in house. As the example of GM shows (see Box 5.14) the management of outsourcing contracts is a long learning process but it can be the right model for companies and a successful one too.

Box 5.13 IT outsourcing could be an issue in a bank merger

In January 2004 JP Morgan Chase & Co. merged with Bank One Corp. and announced that $2.2 bn pre-tax costs savings over a period of three years would result partly as a result of consolidating their respective systems, data centres and IT staffs.

However the question of IT in-sourcing versus outsourcing became a major management issue. The two companies shared different management philosophies and experiences on this topical issue. JP Morgan Chase signed a 7-year outsourcing deal with IBM in 2002 worth $5 bn. By contrast in 2001 Bank One had brought in-house its IT operations from its previous outsourced supplier AT&T.

The strategic decision was made more challenging by the fact that the choice of one option for another will have implications for the IT staff, management hierarchy and the CIOs themselves. Because the banks are not expected to complete their integration until 2007, the role of outsourcing is 'the $64,000 question', said Bill Bradway, a financial analyst.

Source: Hoffman (2004).

Box 5.14 GM's third wave in outsourcing

GM and outsourcing seem to go together. Many people of long standing in the IT industry remember when GM bought Electronic Data Systems Corp. (EDS) in 1984 to run GM's worldwide IT operations under a 10-year $40 bn agreement (first wave of outsourcing). In 1996 GM decided to spin off EDS and started sharing its IT services requirements with other outsourcing suppliers (second wave). Today (2005) GM uses a multitude of suppliers (including all the major outsourcing companies) to manage its IT operations and services (third wave).

According to GM's CIO, Ralph Szygenda, GM has learned a few lessons along the way. 'GM has done things wrong in outsourcing its work, but we changed the model; we did not go back to insource. If you do not put a model in that works, it makes it look like outsourcing does not work. Most companies that switch from outsource to insource is because they typically do not have the right model to manage outsourcing', says Szygenda.

Typical outsourcing mistakes and lessons to learn from GM's experience include:

– do not contract to a single source because the supplier will put its price up and you do not have a competitor
– do not farm out management and IT architectures to a third party
– make sure that you have in-house strategic management to manage the supplier relationships
– put in place a framework that all outsourcers must work with and
– do not let the outsourcing suppliers direct your business.

Continued

Typical benefits form the GM outsourcing experience include;

- \$800 m annual savings in IT costs for the last 7 years
- improved speed and agility for IT decision making and execution
- flexibility to deploy IT resources quickly
- \$1 bn cost reduction in 18 months in business operational efficiencies by using speciality IT service providers.

Source: Hoffman (2003).

Centralised versus decentralised systems

Organisations typically decide on using decentralised IT systems because of their decentralised culture or for geo-political reasons. Other organisations have a strong control culture allowing little or no autonomy to their subsidiaries which supports centralised IT systems. This pattern is highly feasible where all parts of the company operate in the same industry and with very similar business processes. An M&A requires the CIO to take a decision about how best to incorporate the new company into the existing organisation bearing in mind the extent of decentralisation of current and planned IT systems.

Depending on whether the acquired company is being brought into a centralised or a decentralised system, the decision of the CIO needs to consider the potential technical issues associated with each option. For example in a centralised approach, the technical infrastructure will need to be able to cope with typical demands on systems performance, security access, scalability and back-up and recovery from the new subsidiary. From an application viewpoint the technical aspects of the central system would need to take into account the various differences in legal, cultural and user requirements in each country so that the application meets the acquired company's business requirements. User support and help desk provision would need to be considered carefully including language support and time zone differences.

In a decentralised option, the CIO would need to consider technical aspects of allowing a subsidiary to operate its own systems such as network topology, resilience, security access and remote control. From an application view point system interfaces between subsidiary and parent company would become critical for the respective access and interoperability of both systems. User support will continue to be a local issue as before but skill transfer between subsidiary and parent may be necessary to ensure that operating best practices are adopted by both companies.

The management of the IT operation will also differ depending on the option chosen. For example, the question of resources in a decentralised operation is normally left to local management who determines the numbers of IT staff (sometimes agreed with Group CIO and sometimes not) and skills required to support the IT operation. In a centralised operating environment the resource decision is made centrally, sometimes falling short in meeting remote user expectations.

In an M&A situation it is important to have an overall IT strategy within which the debate about how the acquired company is to be integrated can take place. If the parent company has a decentralised strategy to keep using the subsidiary's own systems, integration may be less of an issue than if the group has a centralised policy. Difficulties arise when the parent company wants to install own systems into the subsidiary and the subsidiary wants to keep its systems on grounds of costs, functionality, risk or all three. Sometimes a 'middle of the road' compromise is reached which satisfies both parties. For example keeping some elements of the current system and adopting some from the new parent company. However, while this may be a good compromise solution, the implementation dangers of the so-called best of both worlds approach will be discussed further in Chapter 9.

In a decentralised strategy the initial implementation risks are small. However, in this scenario it is likely that the synergies will also be small. This was the case in C2 where no standard systems at the time of the merger meant the subsidiary was allowed to keep its own system. As a result no real IT synergies were achieved. The same situation happens in a centralised strategy in parent company and a decentralised in subsidiary where the parent company decides for business or technical reasons to leave the decentralised systems in the acquired company. This example is shown in Box 5.15.

Box 5.15   Parent company accepts cheaper local system

In this retail company (C5) the parent company decided to leave the decentralised systems of its newly acquired company alone even though the CIO preferred centralised systems. The reasons were that the parent company's system was too large and costly and not suitable for the small subsidiary. Apart from not being able to support multi-language facilities the parent company's central system would not 'scale down' and it could not run on a smaller company server. Apart from the technical risks the subsidiary system was also more economical to run and met the local requirements much better than the parent company's equivalent.

Source: Extracts from C5.

In a centralised approach the risks are normally higher but these can be minimised at the same time that the synergies are achieved by taking a well-developed and structured approach to integration as is shown in Box 5.11.

Many companies use the decentralised system strategy in an M&A situation by default in order to avoid initial implementation risks. After a

---

Box 5.16   Internal merger of 20 separate business units

C11 is a well known UK-based engineering consultancy firm operating in over 70 countries worldwide. With a turnover of £160 m (2003) and 3,500 staff located in 50+ offices in the UK and overseas C11 has experienced substantial growth and change over the last ten years as a result of both organic growth and multiple acquisitions.

IT has been at the centre of some of these changes. In fact in 1997 when a new IT Director, was appointed the group was very different from what it is today. C11 was then a federation of 20 separate business units. The decentralised culture of the organisation meant that it was not uncommon for several business units to compete for the same client business. The spirit of competition was such that clients were often puzzled by the lack of internal communications among the various business units.

The role of IT in 1997 was also very different. In those days IT was seen as a backroom activity and left to each business unit to decide on hardware and systems. In the words of the IT Director, 'when I arrived in 1997 there were 20 separate systems with virtually no data shared among the business units. The main infrastructure consisted of 2 Novell LAN's in our largest offices and the IT Dept consisted of 20 operations IT staff aided by some engineers part-time'.

Since then the integration of 20 business units into 4 main business groups and 8 world regions has only been possible by the transformation, foresight and support from IT. The IT contribution to the internal merger has indeed been considerable. As the IT Director said: 'as soon as I arrived I realised that I needed to change not only the IT Dept. but the organisation as a whole'. Prompted by the Millennium date requirements the IT Director introduced a standard group accounting system and set about laying the foundation for a standard IT infrastructure.

The IT strategy for merging the disparate business units was developed incrementally. Over a period of 7 years IT moved from a 'free for all' strategy to a standard technology approach based on Microsoft standards. Most of the decisions made 7 years ago have stood the test of time. For example, Dell as the standard desktop PC, IP protocols for the network, Visual Basic (now C# and .NET) as the standard development programming language and so on. These decisions look obvious now but back in 1997 it was a different story.

Source: Extracts from CIO's interview comments.

few acquisitions are added the negative effects can accumulate and cancel out the initial benefits as the following example illustrates, see Box 5.16.

From the above discussion it is clear that deciding on a centralised or decentralised model is a key decision for the CIO. He or she may have to carefully weigh up the different and sometimes conflicting objectives. It is clear that the choice of which computer model has considerable implications for the organisation as a whole. Organisational culture and system models are often linked together for good reasons. Misunderstanding the reason for change could have important organisational, cultural, political and economic risks for the integration project. It is a decision that a wise CIO would want to take with the backing of the entire M&A team.

In-house systems and packages

This issue is similar to the decisions about centralisation or decentralisation in the sense that it relates to the overall IT strategy in both companies. Most companies use standard software packages for their accounting, sales order processing and manufacturing applications. The exception to this is where organisations operate in a very particular field whereby their own in-house developed IT applications give them a competitive advantage.

The most common decision that the CIO will face in relation to packages is, which one? In the situation where the parent company has adopted a particular standard (see below), and the IT software strategy has been agreed upon, it is likely that the parent company's standard package will be used. In today's business world software standardisation is becoming a reality thanks to companies such as Microsoft, SAP and Oracle. Since there is only a handful of tier 1 standard ERP packages to be used this further reduces the potential technology issues. On the other hand, one must always be cautious about labels because, for example, two SAP implementations are never the same. Furthermore, there are a high number of companies that having bought a standard package change it afterwards, making the integration between two SAP systems almost as difficult as two entirely different systems.

A potential issue related to standard package software is the maintenance of the package itself. For example, the CIO may decide to keep their subsidiary's package system only to find out later that the software supplier is no longer supporting that version and that reliance on local IT staff is difficult. Issues such as these can be identified and dealt with effectively if a detailed IT due diligence is performed before the integration starts and emphasise the importance of good information on which the CIO can base M&A decisions.

The question of using an in-house package rather than a standard software package is becoming rarer these days. There is normally a historic reason for the use of such packages, though sometimes there may be an economic or political reason too. In our experience having in-house systems tends to increase costs and risks in the long term, which is paradoxically the opposite of what these systems were often intended to achieve. An in-house package initially appears to be very attractive on cost and timescales. However, the costs of an in-house system tend to increase over time primarily because they are typically designed to meet a particular requirement in a given company at a particular moment in time. They can also be difficult to transport to another organisation without costly modifications. Support risks and costs can be an issue because in-house systems by their nature tend to rely on very specific individuals and these may take advantage of their bargaining position in a change situation. The maintenance can also be expensive and risky if major changes are required.

The key message for the CIO is to insure that the choice of standard package or in-house systems is right. Business requirements and user acceptance should be paramount in helping the CIO to make his or her choice. If the decision is to go for a new package a detailed evaluation process is a must. Consideration must be given to technological obsolescence, supplier support and maintenance costs which are important whatever the choice of new or old. Additionally, if the decision is made on political grounds, for example as part of the deal struck in a merger situation, the CIO should be clear about the long-term implications of this decision and not put him or herself in a position of having to regret it afterwards.

Small company versus big company

In theory the acquisition of a small company should be simple enough from the technological viewpoint. However, this is probably one of the most common types of acquisition or merger where companies underestimate the effort required. Small companies are by nature entrepreneurial and may often cut corners when it comes to business processes, procedures and IT systems. For instance, small companies will often neglect the IT infrastructure, lack written systems documentation, have no formal procedures for dealing with systems testing, and pay little attention to formal training. Such problems are not only limited to small companies but these problems are found more often there than in larger companies. On the plus side a small company's ability to get things up and running quickly at low cost is something that larger parent companies envy and hence find difficult when trying to demonstrate that their own systems are better.

By contrast large companies tend to have organised bureaucracies, apply rules and procedures to most things and in the main have mature and well-developed IT systems and infrastructure. In recent times many large companies have made changes in order to become more nimble by

---

Box 5.17   Pizza tastes better in small bites

Italy

P5 is a household name in UK electronic retail and is looking to expand its European operations. S5 is small and very successful Italian retailer operating in the same business as P5. S5 has a very smart owner who is looking for a buyer. C5 and S5 meet and it is 'love at first sight'. The marriage is agreed and the wedding is arranged.

P5 has had only one other small international acquisition previously and learned that foreign culture and size are key issues in acquisitions so it is determined not to have a problem in this area. S5 being a true Italian company has no previous international experience but likes P5 and assumes that their large size is a reason for P5's success so expects no problem in the integration process. However, just in case, prior to agreeing a full takeover by P5 they agree to live together for a while so they get to know each other better.

The IT due diligence, done by external consultants, started with a detailed assessment of S5's IT organisation, technology and processes, which showed S5's main strengths and weaknesses. Being a small company more preoccupied with opening stores and expanding their sales the whole IT area looks neglected and not much attention has been paid to it. However, close investigation reveals that S5's systems are adequate for their current needs, simple and economic to run even if 10 years old.

By contrast P5's own systems are older, expensive to run and difficult to scale down to be of use for a small company. P5's brand new IT strategy was to develop new group systems and in time move towards standard systems throughout the group. The IT integration team task was to come up with a short-term IT strategy for shoring up S5's current systems and insuring that they could support business growth. A second objective of the integration was to prepare S5 for a smooth integration with P5's systems, processes and technology when these are ready.

Whilst addressing this second objective some of the major challenges facing both companies came to light. The key issues identified were:

- The business culture of the two organisations was very different. P5 was bureaucratic, slow to react and financially driven. By contrast S5 was family-oriented, quick to act and sales oriented.
- Business processes were also very different. P5's processes were supported by well designed systems enhanced over a period of years with strong

Continued

functionality and automation features. By comparison a lot of S5's processes were ad-hoc, non-standard and manually driven.

- Management styles were also very different. P5's managers lacked the entrepreneurial instinct that S5's had. By contrast S5's managers lacked the experience of formal management techniques and found it very difficult to think strategically. For instance, in the area of project management S5's managers lacked formal knowledge and training.
- Decision making processes also reflected the different organisational cultures and where as in P5 major corporate decisions were agreed in formal management committees, in S5 all key decisions were made at individual level, by the previous owner or by the individual manager.
- IT management processes and practices were also different. For instance, in the area of supplier management purchasing of IT products and services in S5 was very informal whereas in the case of P5 the process was very formal and structured.

Source: Extracts from C5.

Box 5.18   Small company bought by larger US group

S9 is a leading independent global provider of private equity investment products and services employing 70 staff and operating in 30 countries. The parent company (P9) is a global leader in investment management employing 1,300 staff and operating in 35 countries. The deal was given the green light by the relevant authorities and completed in February 2004. Four years before S9 had been approached by another company and after 6 months of detailed due diligence the deal was abandoned. This time around S9 knew what to expect out of the IT due diligence and it was prepared.

The parent company had previous acquisition experience and the acquisition of S9 was part of their business strategy. The role of IT in both S9 and P9 is to support the business and although S9 bespoke systems technology is a key differentiator against other competitors the role of IT in the M&A process was a secondary one. P9's IT Director was informed about the acquisition before it was announced publicly. The M&A team was small and the due diligence took 4 months to complete although the actual IT work took only a few weeks.

P9 has adopted a 'leave alone' approach to S9's acquisition and hence the actual IT infrastructure and organisation has been left virtually untouched. The expected IT synergies have been small and reduced mainly to leveraging S9's existing network infrastructure and global purchasing agreements. Both companies use the same type of technology based on Microsoft standards. Email systems and networks have been linked but kept different. S9's technology is considered to be ahead in some areas to that of P9 but in others such as CRM, deal flow and networking P9 has greater capabilities. Being larger in size P9 has also a greater pool of IT resources (200 staff) which S9 may exploit in the future.

The communication process during the acquisition has been straightforward. Being a friendly acquisition and S9 being a small company its culture is very

Continued

open so everyone in S9 was told about the acquisition before it was announced. On the other hand P9 adopted a 'need to know' policy approach with only a few senior managers knowing before it was announced. From an IT perspective given the small IT team involved S9 did not have any major issues in this area.

So far there have not been any major cultural issues although the difference in size between the two companies means that some of the management processes are different. For example, taking a decision involves more people and takes longer now that before the acquisition. S9's IT Director explained that whereas before he could make decisions fairly quickly now he has to consult a number of P9 IT managers before he can proceed.

Although both companies are international in scope there have not been any major issues to do with language, geography or foreign culture. The 'leave alone' strategy adopted has meant that S9's international operation has not been substantially affected.

Because the acquisition is very recent it is too early to draw any major conclusions and learning points. It appears that the 'leave alone' approach adopted by P9 has so far produced only benefits and both companies expect to continue to enjoy the "honeymoon" period for a little longer.

Source: Extracts from financial company CIO's interview – C9.

Box 5.19 UK software company bought by US group

S12 is a small UK software company specialising in on-line fault detection and monitoring software using artificial intelligence based technologies. P12 is a US company comprising five diverse, multi-national companies with a network of 30 locations worldwide.

The acquisition strategy was developed after a successful joint marketing agreement between the two companies after which P12 decided to buy S12. The acquisition rational being that the intelligent software produced by S12 identifies the business opportunities for the hardware work that P12 performs.

The role of IT during the acquisition process was not significant because of the relatively small size of S12 (10 staff) and the 'leave alone and nurture' approach adopted by P12. The IT due diligence process was limited to a formal visit by P12's Head office IT management when S12's accounting, HR and email systems were reviewed. A year after the acquisition the email and HR systems were changed but the accounting systems remained as before.

The communication process during the acquisition was slightly different in each company. S12 communicated to its employees the formal acquisition by P12 early in the process and it was not a surprise as the acquisition followed the joint marketing agreement between the two companies. In the case of P12 being a larger and publicly quoted company and due to confidential reason only a handful of senior managers were informed before the acquisition became public.

Continued

Given the very entrepreneurial culture of both companies and the stand-off approach taken by P12 there were no significant cultural issues during the acquisition process. To help the transition process S12's MD role was an important one. He acted as a bridge between the UK and US cultures as he had studied and lived in the US and understood well the American culture. 'In the UK we have an international outlook and this has also facilitated the communications within P12's international network', he said.

No external IT consultants were used. Only an external lawyer was required during the acquisition process.

According to S12's MD the key lessons learned from the acquisition are: do not change business operating practices unless they are needed and when you do take time to plan them and execute them properly. For example, taking time to change the email avoided unnecessary errors and got everyone's cooperation. It seems that the nurturing and caring approach adopted by P12 has produced the expected results 3 years after the acquisition was completed.

Source: Extracts from CIO's interview – C12.

Box 5.20   Acquisition in the publishing industry

S15 is a small independent and successful publisher operating in Europe, USA and Asia. P15 is the business-to-business division of a world leader in the publishing industry. S15 fits P15's acquisition rationale in terms of product, market and skills and the deal is completed swiftly.

The communication process within IT was difficult at the beginning. There was a question of trust between the existing IT staff and the new IT Director and establishing the initial rapport took time. This was overcome by open communications with regular meetings and personal incentives including training and career development. Special care was needed in those cases where employees had particular technical skills which were critical for the successful continuation of the business operation.

Some cultural issues were also experienced during the integration process. These had to do with the difference in size between the two companies but also with different organisational cultures. For example, P15 brought some well-tested processes for decision making that S15's staff felt were too bureaucratic. By contrast P15 management felt that S15's small company culture was too limiting and close knit.

In the international scene there were fewer issues. Language was not a problem and because a decision was made to leave the previous overseas management in place no major change was experienced. This decision was seen later as a potential mistake because to get things done differently required a considerable amount of P15's management own time far in excess to anything anticipated at the beginning of the acquisition.

Continued

The use of external consultants was considered unnecessary because P15 felt that they had the necessary skills in-house. However, the due diligence exercise failed to identify serious risks and in retrospect this may have been also a mistake. According to the IT Director 'having consultants that have done this type of exercise before is very valuable and avoids falling into traps that are inevitable when one makes an acquisition for the first time. You need a forensic type of approach which is difficult to find in a normal IT Dept.', he said.

The key learning points to remember from S15's experience are:

1. Carry out IT due diligence properly and thoroughly. This enables the identification of risks, opportunities and also the possibility of pulling out of the deal before is too late.
2. Do not underestimate the time taken to make M&A work. Do not be deceived by the size of the transaction either. A small acquisition does not mean less work and less management time.
3. The 'softly-softly' integration approach can work and is good when the business that you are buying is profitable.
4. Be prepared to be creative in the way that you compensate and retain IT staff with special skills.

Source: Extracts from CIO's interview from C15.

reducing layers of management and simplifying processes. Nevertheless, the differences between such organisations and particularly small start-ups and other entrepreneurial businesses that they may acquire are significant and can become potential roadblocks to IT integration in an M&A.

The example shown in Box 5.17 illustrates that when confronted with differences in culture, business processes, management practices and technology, parent companies may take the decision to go 'slowly' in the integration and take small 'bites' rather than going for sweeping changes. A similar approach was taken by the parent companies illustrated in Boxes 5.18 and 5.19.

The example of the case shown in Box 5.20 illustrates a slightly different and also successful approach. It is interesting to notice that in this case study the CIO makes the points that 'small acquisitions do not take less time than large ones'. The other point about this case is the question of retaining key staff. Retaining key IT staff after a merger is always an issue, but in the case of a small company bought by a large one, this is more of an issue because of the additional cultural differences. People that like working for small companies often find it very difficult working for large companies as they feel they lose their sense of identity.

From a CIO's viewpoint the key message is not to underestimate the integration challenges of small companies and plan appropriately. The cultural question should also be assessed with care as working with small companies requires a different approach to dealing with people issues. For example, the vulnerability to someone leaving who has special technical knowledge of how the local system operates would leave the CIO more exposed than in a larger IT department.

6
Management Issues

The CIO has a dual management responsibility in an M&A: on the one hand he or she should be part of the senior management team responsible for decisions about the transaction as a whole; on the other hand the CIO has to manage directly the integration of the IT function across the organisations involved in the deal. A survey of senior managers reported by Roythorn (1997) noted that the key lessons respondents learned from their involvement in M&As revolved around planning. Planning should have been done earlier and more efficiently and should include thorough due diligence. The other point emphasised was to recognise what you do not know or cannot do and to seek help promptly.

The interviews with CIOs supported the crucial role of early involvement and planning. However, they also emphasised that while planning is vital, the role of CIO in integration is much broader than that of a planner. The CIO has to be a strategist, a leader, and a communicator working with stakeholders inside and outside the IT department and the firm. He or she will also at times have a hands-on role in the integration project.

Good management practices on the part of the CIO and team are vital to the mitigation of IT risk in an M&A. In this chapter we discuss some of the typical management issues that a CIO or IT manager will face in an M&A. The selection of which management issues are more important than others depends on the nature of the M&A. However, the top 10 selected here, and shown in Box 6.1 are likely to need attention to a greater or lesser extent in every M&A a CIO is faced with.

Strategy and leadership

Agreeing the IT synergies

IT synergies may or may not be clear after the M&A is announced but the first thing that the CIO must do is to agree them with the business.

Box 6.1   Top 10 IT management issues

1. Agreeing the IT synergies
2. Creating a shared vision
3. Leading the change
4. Planning and organising
5. Selecting the M&A IT team
6. Retaining key skills
7. Dealing with cultural issues
8. Managing communications
9. Dealing with suppliers/customers
10. Review processes and learning points

Box 6.2   Providing day one service

Between 1997 and 2002 Intel acquired over 40 companies. To be able to handle the integration activities the company created its own M&A IT team. To address the connectivity issue Intel developed a quick and easy PC-based routing and access solution called the 'pocket network solution'. This solution implemented in 80% of the acquired companies, which include international sales offices, is part of the Day 1 Services. Day 1 Services include a menu of networked connectivity items and access to Intel applications. As a second step a leased line is offered to the HQ of the acquired company. The last step is the final connection to one of the nearest Intel sites in the region of the acquired company (this last step takes several months)

Source: Intel (2002).

If the M&A deal has been well planned and structured an official statement will exist about what IT synergies are expected and in what timeframe. If it does not exist, the equivalent must be created. The next thing that the CIO must do is to agree priorities with the business. Lack of clarity in what is to be achieved increases risk. There will be key operational priorities that are entirely in the hands of IT, and quick wins which need to be coordinated with the business. Day One connectivity is generally crucial: 'Establishing seamless e-mail, intranet and file transfer is vital for smooth operations. Other items that require early close attention are security, help-desk and legal and contractual issues' (Popovich 2001). This is illustrated in Box 6.2

In parallel with operational changes to the IT infrastructure the CIO will be addressing short-term quick wins. These are priorities identified by the senior management in their official M&A announcement and typically involve rationalisation programmes such as headcount reductions, and cancellation of duplicated or unwanted services and supplier contracts. At this point decisions have to be made on re-location of services, people and infrastructure. Outsourcing deals may also need to be negotiated with suppliers.

An issue for the CIO is to balance speed versus quality of execution. In the case of C17 the CIO went to considerable lengths to strike this balance: 'We have to keep the balance between speed and quality because in our industry IT represents 25–30% of the M&A synergies and 50% of the total integration costs. If we rush things and our quality process are not followed the relationship between IT synergies and IT costs will suffer. We take the time to ensure that this balance is right' (utilities business CIO comments).

Speed of execution is clearly an important driver in most M&As. In a study reported by Savill and Wright (2002) it was found that companies which managed the process of integration on a fast track basis achieved higher levels of profitability, productivity, cash flow and gross margins.

Over time the concept of speed gains in importance for senior management. A CEO in the investment banking field was quoted as saying: 'You can get away with anything on Day One, less so in Day Two and people get most upset as time goes on' (Savill and Wright 2002). For reasons of both speed and quality the CIO and his IT team must work very closely with the business to extract the synergy value and make timely decisions. An example of how a CIO dealt with this issue is shown in Box 6.3.

The CIO should be aware of the problems that may ensue if, in order to meet business requirements, an increase is proposed in the scope of change beyond that required to implement the integration of the two organizations' IT functions. This point was clearly made in discussion with one of the CIO's in our research. 'Resist the temptation of making any major functionality enhancements when integrating the two companies, because it will increase the risks and costs' (utilities business CIO comments).

Box 6.3 Don't let business departments hold up IT integration

In the merger of Go and easy-Jet, IT Manager Blair Stewart needed to get some decisions made by the business before he could proceed with some of the IT integration work. 'Push them (business) as hard as you can to make their key decisions. We could not start any IT planning until we knew them. Forcing requirements out of them was vital', he said. Two key decisions that were affecting IT were the location of the new head office and whether easy-Jet's reservation system was going to have to change to accommodate differences in Go's product. To solve this issue Stewart assigned an IT account manager to liaise with each business department.

Source: Vowler (2003).

In any integration a balance needs to be struck between short-term and long-term integration objectives. Timescales may dictate certain projects in a given timeframe. The CIO must set the right expectations and meet them. He will be judged on both IT synergies and IT integration costs and to be successful he needs the agreement and support from the business. Inevitably, some amount of horse-trading will also be necessary in order to arrive at an optimum plan for integration acceptable to both the business and IT.

Creating a shared vision

Where two IT departments are to merge creating a shared vision is essential. Regardless of the approach to IT integration that has been chosen (centralisation or decentralisation, single standards or multiple systems) the CIO will need to create a common vision of the future that is bought into by both IT departments.

Along with the chosen strategic approach to integration, a number of other key decisions need to be made involving people, systems, and location of services. Articulating a clear vision that is transmitted through clear and open communications helps to keep uncertainty to a minimum. Uncertainty cannot be eliminated altogether because it is part of the process although it may seem particularly disturbing to those involved in an M&A for the first time. Two examples of how CIOs have dealt with integrating two IT departments and activities are shown in Boxes 6.4 and 6.5.

In each case a clear underpinning message about the future was communicated to those involved. In the first example IT successfully used the CEO's communication messages to re-enforce the need for change. In the second example the CIO used the clear agreed strategic objectives to similarly drive the IT changes required. He was also very conscious of the cultural differences between the two organisations and used the local language to establish a good rapport and cooperation from the acquired company business and IT staff.

A shared vision can be fostered by having a clear integration strategy, cultural empathy and open communications. Another important aspect of creating a shared vision is selling the benefits. However, corporate selling messages about 'two companies united are better than two separate ones' are prone to scepticism. To be successful the CIO needs to do his or her homework beforehand and get to know the people that he or she is dealing with. In some cases the fact that people may save their jobs by cooperating and as a result they may be considered as part of the future IT organisation is a good start. Additionally, personal benefits such as training and better career prospects may also predispose people

Box 6.4 Merging two IT departments: public company

C14 is the result of the merger of two leading NHS Trusts in the UK. Prior to 1998, the two organisations provided separate patient services and treatments across a large city. Today c14 is probably the largest NHS Trust in the UK, employing 16,000 staff across eight sites and treating 210,000 inpatients (including 60,000 day cases), and 730,000 outpatients each year. It has more than 3,000 beds and an annual budget of about £600 million.

The rationale for the merger came about as a result of the UK government political agenda to improve the services and efficiencies of the NHS. The strategic objectives were threefold: 1. comply with UK Government directive, 2. increase efficiency, and 3. decrease clinical risks.

The IT involvement started well before the merger was announced. At the request of one of the two IT Directors (he later became the IT Director of the merged organisation) the two IT Departments got together and started discussing ways of exchanging information. This early planning and foresight enabled c14 to deploy a common email system to 4,500 staff only 2 days after the merger was implemented. This same initiative had already delivered a single common telephone system, and subsequently led to a common IT and network infrastructure and integrated systems.

The communication process worked well within the two IT organisations coming together. The early planning and involvement from both IT departments paid off, and some of the technical and cultural differences were resolved early in the integration process. Some management techniques, such as a new IT organisation with an even balance from members of the two previous constituent organisations, new training, and career development, also helped to keep the IT staff turnover low. Some of the IT success has been copied later by other departments where the integration has proved more difficult.

The cultural issues were also handled very well, with the CEO setting the rules at the very beginning of the merger process. 'The policy of being seen to be fair actually worked', says the IT Director.

Source: Health sector CIO's comments.

Box 6.5 Merging IT activities: private company

S10 is a German producer of plastic sheeting owned by a large international group. P10 is a large division of a major UK Plc in the chemical industry. In 1998 P10 acquires S10 in order to extend its market and production facilities. Its manufacturing facility located in East Germany had a total number of 200 staff. P10 is a large corporate with more than 35,000 staff worldwide.

From the beginning of the acquisition the IT strategic objectives were clearly defined. These included the integration of the key processes: supply chain, marketing and production. The role of IT was critical to identify the IT technical risks and to prepare the organisation for the implementation of a

Continued

new ERP system based on SAP technology. The work required to streamline the business processes was also very important in order to take advantage of SAP functionality.

The IT technology model used for the integration was a mixture of local systems (already running before the acquisition and related to the factory processes) and those adopted by the parent company (mainly in the business and dispatch areas). The integration of the first phase of the project took 6 months approximately with the implementation of SAP 3 months later.

The communication and cultural aspects of the project were also crucial. The importance of regular, minuted project meetings attended by all the key stakeholders was a great contributor to the success of the integration project. Another essential ingredient was to speak German. All communications were in fact in German and that helped to get everyone behind the project and know what was expected from them. The face to face communications were essential especially at the beginning of the project to create rapport and generate support for the project.

Source: Manufacturing business CIO's comments.

to accept change. The question of 'what is in it for me?' always helps to focus on the right agenda for the CIO.

A technique that one of the authors has used successfully in the past when merging two separate IT departments is to spend sometime together with the two IT departments analysing the past achievements. After that do the same with the weaknesses. Finally build a vision where the combined IT departments move forward and learn from each other's experience and build a new stronger department with more strengths and fewer weaknesses. The approach is to be honest and build trust to get everybody involved and genuinely learn about people's expectations of building a new future where everyone feels that they have got something to gain rather than lose.

The ideal is to create a shared vision of the future but in some cases this is not possible and the best that can be achieved is a clear vision of what needs to be done. Company culture, management philosophy and management practices in the companies to be joined may be very different. They need to be recognised and discussed so that major differences can be bridged to allow effective integration to take place. The question of control may also be relevant, for example when dealing with small companies where a great deal of autonomy may have been given in the past. In such situations the CIO needs to be honest and explain what realistically can and cannot be expected in the new regime.

Leading the change

Poor leadership is often the single most significant reason for mergers to fail. In our own experience when we look back and see the outcome of the multiple mergers that we have been involved with, the most successful ones have always had a strong leader who drove the whole merger process from beginning to end. Strong leadership also means being able to identify, understand and appreciate the strengths and weaknesses in both organisations. Strong leadership and smart management will recognise that neither organisation is perfect and it is the combination of the best practices from both that delivers results.

Merger success depends greatly on leading and managing people. No matter what the rationale for the merger is, its success depends to a large extent on the M&A leader who will take control and lead from the front throughout the entire process. The leader must show enthusiasm, drive, and determination for achieving the strategic objectives. It must be clear to everyone who is in charge and he or she must have his or her accountability and reward linked to the success of the merger. It is no good just being involved at the pre-acquisition stage and then delegate to others later. He or she must lead all the way until the end of the process.

Examples of successful leadership in successful M&As are shown below in Boxes 6.6 and 6.7.

In the same way as there must be a good leader in the business the CIO needs to take the leadership role as far as the IT work is concerned. Leading change involves understanding not only the IT but also the

---

Box 6.6   Leadership in the oil industry

After the BP Amoco merger BP's CEO Sir John Browne created a $200 Billion integrated energy company. His leadership also achieved $2 Billion cost savings in the first year and he also succeeded in creating a single organisation with common standard and values.

Source: Gadiesh *et al.* (2002).

Box 6.7   Leadership in the packaging industry

Rolf Borjesson CEO of Rexam created an international leader in the package industry using a series of acquisitions to increase scale while simultaneously selling units that not longer fit his model.

Source: Gadiesh *et al.* (2002).

organisation as a whole. 'As soon as I arrived I realised that I needed to change not only the IT department but the organisation as a whole' (engineering consultancy CIO comments). In an M&A there will always be people that are reluctant to change. The CIO needs to understand the political environment in which he or she is moving and generate support from the key stakeholders in order to drive change. The main difference for the CIO between normal operation and M&A work is that in the M&A context many key stakeholders are new and he or she will need to build new relationships at a time when people are uncertain about the future.

One of the difficulties that the CIO may find in this process is that levels of cooperation may be poor because of fear of job losses or just plain uncertainty, particularly if the acquisition is an unfriendly one. In these situations it is also important to recognise the personal, political and emotional aspects. Concentrating on planned and rational aspects of integration ignores the latter. Staff in the acquired company may feel defeated and defensive, which can lead to withdrawal and indifference or active resistance and even sabotage.

In the IT arena once the decision about which systems to keep and which ones to discard has been made a number of other decisions follow:

- Who do we need to keep, who can we let go?
- How long do we need to keep certain people?
- How do we keep the people that we want to keep?
- In which way are we going to transition the systems?
- Do we have the right technical expertise to support the legacy systems if people from the acquired company go?

In a situation where both systems are to be kept the issues are easier. If only one system is to remain, getting the buy-in from the other party to staff changes may be more difficult. Discussing and agreeing the IT strategy with the other party helps the change process. The CIO also needs to exercise flexibility in how the change is done without compromising his or her own objectives. During this change process the CIO will be putting his or her own credibility on the line and in order to succeed he or she will need experience, to generate trust and be lucky, preferably all three.

Planning, management and communications

Planning and organising

The integration plan is arguably the cornerstone of the acquisition process. Without a plan it is not possible to know the destination, the direction and the various routes to get there. It is the map! In a way the integration plan is like the DNA of the M&A. By looking at the plan the experienced manager or consultant can see very quickly the type of M&A that is involved.

A good IT implementation plan must be an integral part of the overall M&A integration plan. An inadequate integration plan is one of the reasons for cost escalation, delays and failures. Unfortunately, some companies are not good at planning. There is the real case of a company where one of the authors worked as a consultant where the CEO felt that planning was a ploy for consultants to make money. He told his staff to do their M&A tasks as part of their day-to-day activities because he believed the integration work should take only 4 weeks to complete. Needless to say the integration was not a success because it needed more time and a better coordinated approach. Although this may be an extreme case, experience from our research shows that companies that have a good integration plan and execute it well are clear winners in the M&A business. This point is corroborated time and again by CIOs (see Box 6.8).

Most CIOs are not new to planning or to project management but a lack of previous M&A experience can give rise to a number of difficulties when undertaking integration activities. The amount of activity to be completed in a very short space of time and the high profile nature of the work requires the best project management skills. The aim is to have as complete plan as possible before the integration is started. If this is not possible then stringent and professional project management is even more essential to make up for lost time.

A challenge in the planning and organising process is the amount of resources needed, where to get them from and how to make best use of them. A skills inventory will indicate which skills are essential to keep

---

Box 6.8   CIO's comments about the importance of planning

'Get the IT integration plan ready and implement it as soon as possible. If not in place after six months integration issues, particularly people issues, become more difficult'. (C16)

'Prepare a detailed activity plan with Day 1 activities all the way to 12 months later activities'. (C10)

'Have a clear M&A IT plan before merger starts by including IT in the due diligence'. (C1)

'Have a clear IT M&A plan (i.e. do not make it up as you go along)'. (C2)

'Implement fast but plan and execute properly (i.e. do not rush, the risks are higher than the rewards)'. (C3)

from the new company. Key individuals that need to be retained will be expecting assurances that they are needed for the long term rather than just for completing the integration work so effective communications, trust and contractual negotiations will need to be in place to succeed.

The CIO must have an overall plan that is realistic and achievable with the available resources and time and budget constraints. Planned activities have both a time aspect and a cost. And planning will involve trade-offs between the two. Integration plan and budget are the key management tools that the CIO is responsible for. Associated with them there is the question of planning methodology and standards. In a complex integration with many planned activities, for example, the merger of RBS and NatWest a robust planning methodology is needed. Typically this may be PRINCE2, a process-based approach for project management. PRINCE was first developed by the Central Computer and Telecommunications Agency (ACTA) now part of Office of Government Commerce (OCG) in 1989 as a UK Government standard for IT project management. In small or medium projects other planning tools such as Microsoft Project will be adequate. (Note: this discussion on the integration plan is continued in the next chapter.)

Although the issue of culture is dealt with separately below, it is relevant to note that there are different approaches to planning depending on culture. For example, the concept of time is an interesting one. From the experience of several M&As projects that have involved German or US companies it is clear that in these cultures the concept of time has been taken very seriously. For example, if an activity in the integration plan was behind this would be a serious matter in these cultures. By contrast in another acquisition project where a Malaysian company was involved the fact that they were falling behind the plan was not seen as a serious matter. The reason was that the concept of time is seen differently by different cultures. In the Anglo-Saxon and German cultures formality is important and time is part of it. In the Malaysian culture time is one of the few things in life freely available and therefore is to be enjoyed and not measured in the same degree (Gancel *et al.* 2002). As one of the CIOs remarked in an interview: 'In UK culture broad headings are good enough; in German culture detailed plans are expected.'

Selecting the M&A IT team

A number of different teams need to be created to carry through the integration of a merged or acquired company. In building the integration team resources should include people from both companies and external consultants if required. An important point to remember here is that target company resources may not stay long after the acquisition so careful selection of the target company management and staff is necessary.

The IT integration team should be part of the wider mergers and acquisition team. The latter must have a management group responsible for setting the direction, initial goals, priorities and evaluating the changes and integration process as it progresses. In addition to the management team there should also be cross-functional operating teams. Depending on the type and culture of the organisation IT may be one of those teams on its own or imbedded into the business teams. Typically, these will be organised either by business units, functions or specific integration projects (see Figure 6.1). The operating team members should be people with the best knowledge from parent, subsidiary or external consultants where additional expertise is required. This is a good opportunity for fast-track career development as the integration work presents a good opportunity to get to know the business and form new relationships with peers, management and staff.

In selecting the team the question of skills is essential. Depending on the strategy and size of the project the CIO will need to rely on key technical, project management and business skills. The technical skills will depend on the technology used and on the integration option chosen.

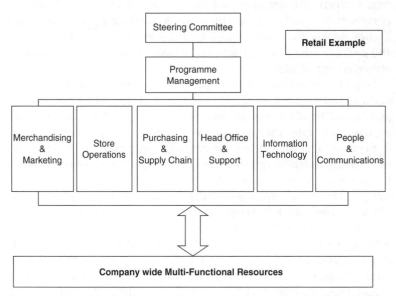

. . . Structured around synergies and using the best knowledge and skills available

Figure 6.1   M&A integration organisation

If the option is to put the parent company's systems in, then most of the expertise will be expected from them. On the other hand if a 'best of breed' option is chosen then a combination of the two companies IT will be required. In any case, it is always good to have a mixed team from both companies to understand each other's business processes and work towards a full integration. The project manager(s) will ideally need to be a 'heavy weight', very experienced in the business, in project management and have had previous experience of mergers and acquisitions IT, where necessary at an international level.

Where teams are to operate across borders, a number of additional factors must be taken into account. One such factor is the choice of the working language. If English is not the natural language for both companies a decision must be taken regarding the working language. Finding bilingual people with the right technical skills will add time to the project. International mergers and acquisitions require specific skills. Internationalism is not achieved simply by a mixture of different nationalities put together in an integration project. Staff are needed who are multi-lingual, have work experience in countries outside their own, and knowledge of conducting international business and working in multi-cultural environments. Multi-lingual, IT technologists and application experts are not easy to find. The use of experienced external IT consultants can be a good alternative in meeting a particular IT skill in short supply. Companies that have HR policies that recognise, recruit and promote international talent find it easier to manage the integration of foreign subsidiaries.

A decision must be taken about what size the team should be? The size of the IT team is based on many factors such as company practice, complexity and size of the merger, and the CIO's style. Best practices indicate a group of not more than 5–10 people who form the core of the IT team. It is essential that these people are carefully selected and have all the relevant skills and credibility to command the support from both companies. In general, experience shows that if you have fewer people involved things get done more efficiently than if you have tens of people involved.

A key success factor is to combine the right IT technical and business application skills with good inter-personal skills. The CIO needs to achieve the integration objectives foremost but at the same time he should be aiming to build a new team with resources from both companies for the longer term. Integration provides a good opportunity to test individual team member's ability to work together. The balance and the chemistry of the chosen members are important to success. Similarly appearing to be objective and fair in the assessment of the chosen members will be well received. The CIO's early decisions on team formation will be watched by both sides with a great deal of attention, especially by both IT departments.

Retaining key skills

Retaining key IT skills in the post-merger integration is one of the key issues for CIOs. There is plenty of evidence that suggests that people have a tendency to leave the new organisation if they are not 'looked after' in the way that they expect. One American study carried out by American Management Association says that 'one out of four top performers leaves the company within 3 months of the announcement of an event involving major change in the organisation and 47 per cent of senior managers leave within the first year' (Key Strategy 2003).

Experienced IT people are particularly difficult to replace. For example, people with experience of key legacy systems are unlikely to be available in the market place at short notice. To avoid this situation the CIO needs to plan ahead, ascertain quickly the key people to be retained, and have open and clear discussions with them. Open communications with and reassurance that their skills are recognised and valued must be followed by building the trust and showing integrity to make the CIO's offer appear credible. This can be assisted by getting them involved in the integration process and offering them the opportunity to contribute with their views. Key staff should be prioritised for support to help integration offered by HR and personal needs should be taken into account by negotiating the right contract and benefits.

In the example below the CIO dealt successfully with the issue of retaining key staff by recognising the quality of the existing staff and systems. As a result he managed to keep the IT Manager which in turn influenced the acquired company staff to stay (see Box 6.9).

Box 6.9   Retaining IT staff: oil company

The communication process played its role in the success of the acquisition. Although the M&A strategy was clear to everyone it was necessary to overcome the natural uncertainty about job losses. The IT Manager in charge of the integration project (the same manager in charge of the Italian project IT Management in C16) got down quickly to work and reassured his new IT staff (including the IT Manager from the acquired company who was retained) that job losses would be based on a voluntary basis and with the usually generous competitive company leaving benefits. This approach meant that the two IT teams got to work in a cooperative way and the integration plan was quickly agreed and acted upon. Care was also taken to recognise the quality of the IT staff and systems of the acquired company even though C16 systems and standards were to be implemented.

Source: Oil business CIO's comments.

> *Box 6.10*   Retaining IT staff: publishing company
>
> The communication process within IT was difficult at the beginning. There was a question of trust between the existing IT staff and the new IT Director and establishing the initial rapport took time. This was overcome by open communications with regular meetings and personal incentives including training and career development. Special care was needed in those cases where employees had particular technical skills which were critical for the successful continuation of the business operation.
>
> *Source*: Publishing business CIO's comments.

In the second case, the CIO dealt successfully with the issue by a combination of building personal trust with the new team and providing appropriate new contractual terms that made the idea of staying attractive.

Dealing with cultural issues

'Culture can be a major obstacle to change and is often the main culprit in the failure of corporate deals. Managing the cultural component of integration is critical to success' (Gancel 2002). However culture is a difficult concept to understand and work with. 'Culture is essentially a shorthand term' (Lee 2003). It is a convenient way of grouping different and difficult concepts such values, beliefs, language, religion, corporate culture, customs and practice and many others.

In certain cultures individual beliefs and values are very strong. In others the group and team values dominate. In a merger of two US companies, which ultimately failed, one of the reasons given for failure was that the acquired company's senior managers and scientists pulled out shortly after the parent company announced their merger plans because they felt that their individual position would suffer. In other words corporate objectives were, they felt, against their own personal objectives. By contrast in a small Italian company where the founder and previous owner had instilled a 'paternalistic' and family culture, the parent company decided after the merger to retain the owner as the CEO and no staff left. A year later the CEO then retired and still no one left. The family value that he had inspired lived much longer than anyone, including the parent company, had anticipated. The group values prevailed over the individual values.

Differences in corporate culture, in underlying values and in ways of working, may also pose a challenge. 'Organisational cultures don't export and transplant easily' (Lee 2003). Incompatible organisational cultures may be a result of operating in different businesses. They also occur between different business functions and between different professions and management styles. Such differences need to be identified early in the integration process and taken account of in preparing the merger strategy. The risk of ignoring such differences is that integration plans will found or on misunderstanding and conflict.

Culture is important in all types of mergers and acquisitions but it is in the international M&A environment that cultural questions rooted in nationality, language and different customs and values are likely to be most profound. The combination of these additional factors adds complexity to the work that the CIO needs to accomplish in cross-border integrations. Such challenges come in all shapes and sizes. A significant challenge would be for the CIO to be tasked with a large merger of two different international manufacturing groups with their own established markets operating in 15 countries, using 12 different languages, different IT technology developed locally and using their own local management practices in a decentralised non-compatible IT environment. On the surface a small 'across the border' English acquisition of a Scottish manufacturing assembly company would be much simpler. Yet the two examples in reality were similar in that they involved an integration approach that was to a great extent driven by the cultural phenomenon.

Where national cultures are based on very different or incompatible values and assumptions M&A integration is particularly difficult. For example, Japanese take a strategic view of things, prefer a centralised type of organisation and are driven by team work and consensus. US companies on the other hand are short term, financially oriented, comfortable with a decentralised organisation, driven by individualism and task-oriented (Child 2003). In a merger between companies with these roots a very high degree of cultural sensitivity and compromise is needed to succeed.

Simple misunderstandings about local customs and practices can also lead to problems. In an acquisition some years ago involving a UK company (the parent company) and a Japanese company the newly appointed British General Manager (GM) in charge of the Japanese subsidiary wanted to get payroll information from his new company. He knew that the Japanese company had its payroll done outside by another company but he wanted to bring this information in-house so he had more control over it. Consequently, he asked the integration team to write the relevant conversion software to transfer this information from the outside supplier. When this task was investigated it turned out that the third party supplier had a semi-manual system that delivered the payslips by a man on his bike at the end of each month. When the GM was told about it he could not believe it, and said: 'I asked my Japanese finance manager about his payroll system and he said that it was very good and that it was used by many other local companies, so I assumed it was on a computer somewhere.' What the GM had failed to understand was that at that time Japanese companies did not always trust computers when it came to personal information and 'the man on his bike' was seen as far more secure and reliable.

Language has already been noted as an important dimension of international M&As. It is generally accepted that English is the language of the business world and certainly of the world of IT. However, imposing English in preference to the local national language brings practical issues in the integration process. For example, in a recent merger of an Italian company with its English parent, although a number of senior managers used English, it was found that the IT Manager and 90 per cent of his staff did not speak English. By being able to carry out the integration activities in Italian everyone involved understood what needed to be done and why and hence the buy-in was much better. Having to carry out the same exercise in English would have been more difficult and would not have achieved the same results in time and within the allocated budget. However, this was the only example among the interviews where a language other than English was used for the integration. Using English as the translation language can also add costs as in Box 6.11

The reliance on English as the language used for communications has other dimensions. Because most companies' senior and middle managers speak good English, language appears not to be a problem among people from different nationalities. However, language is a key factor in terms of trust (essential ingredient for team work and cooperation) and control of information. A common language can conceal differences in meaning as shown in Box 6.12.

Box 6.11   The importance of local language

An English GM with a Japanese parent company complained that all written communication coming from Japan was in Japanese and therefore this was a problem for him. If he wanted to know what the documents were saying he needed a translation.

Source: Child *et al.* (2003).

Box 6.12 Same language, different culture

I find American business culture pretty difficult. Our UK former parent company never talked about caring and valuing people but its actions showed that it did. Our new US parent company talks a huge amount about caring and valuing people but when the going gets tough ... It doesn't care at all.

Source: Child *et al.* (2003).

Cultural differences can have a direct impact on IT systems and on the question of which best practices to use. The idea of using international best practices is a good one but they need to be applied in the local context. Working as an independent consultant in a recent merger involving a Greek company one of the authors was able to apply some of the best practices developed by the UK parent company for the assessment of the IT function. At one point during the evaluation of the local systems a particular local practice involving customer discounts that was outside the corporate guidelines was noted. When the reason for this practice was discovered it came to light that this was part of the way Greek customers buy products and imbedded in the relationship of customer and supplier going back many years and essential to retain customer loyalty. It also highlighted a clever way of using discounting techniques in IT systems. The parent company was very impressed and changed their group IT system to include this local practice which is now part of the new updated group standards. The decision to do this while applying best practices was a question of balance and pragmatism which brought benefit to both companies.

The interviews with CIOs illustrated the different approaches that can be taken to integration in the face of differences in culture stemming from nationality, size, industry background and history. The outcome, as shown in Table 6.1 was that 50 per cent of the companies adopted the parent company's system, 35 per cent a mixture of the two and 15 per cent left the acquired system the same.

As a result some acquired companies found themselves adopting in its entirety the parent company's model and with it their culture and IT systems. Although all of them were successful, the loss of personality and positive characteristics within the acquired company was one of the results. An example of this is shown in Box 6.13.

Table 6.1   Survey: cultural issues and how they were addressed

Company Ref.	Cultural issues encountered			How they were addressed
	Culture	Size	Nationality	
C6	√	√		Adopted parent co. culture with centralised standard IT model
C7	√	√	√	Adopted parent co. culture and standard IT model
C9	√	√	√	Acquired company left unchanged
C10	√		√	Best of both, use of local language, standard IT systems
C11	√	√		Greater coordination amongst units with centralised standard IT model
C12	√	√	√	Acquired company left unchanged
C13	√	√	√	Different approaches: either decentralised to preserve M&A value or centralised to achieve economies of scale
C14	√		√	Political objective, common IT system
C15	√			Adopted parent co. culture and IT systems
C16	√	√	√	Adopted parent co. culture and IT systems
C17	√	√	√	Adopted parent co. culture and IT systems
C18	√	√	√	Adopted parent co. and IT systems

Box 6.13   Parent company imposes own culture

In the merger of BP–Amoco, CEO, John Browne shows how he dealt success-fully with the initial cultural misalignment of the two companies by choosing one culture. BP's assimilation of Amoco was so complete that it gave rise to a running joke: 'question: how do you pronounce BP Amoco? Answer: BP. The Amoco is silent'. Having taken a hands-off approach to previous acquisitions which were costly he stated: 'I learned that you have to have clarity with an acquisition. You can't let things work themselves out'. The process of integra-tion created value for the shareholders measured in terms of BP Amoco stock. price, which rose nearly 11% during the initial 11-day period of the merger. (Vestring *et al.* 2003).

Cultural issues are always a factor in M&A, particularly in international transactions. The CIO has to deal with the interaction of cultural factors with IT issues such as the use of different technology platforms in the merging companies. CIOs that plan for these issues before the merger is started come out more successfully than those that are unaware, ignore them or consider them as afterthought. In international mergers and acquisitions using experienced international resources with multilingual and multicultural backgrounds increases the chances of being successful by anticipating and addressing the cultural and linguistic integration issues. Cultural integration takes a long time but it is not an excuse for leaving it at the mercy of post integration events.

Managing communications

'Poor communications between people at all levels of the organisation, and between the two organisations that are merging, is one of the principal reasons why mergers fail' (Key Strategy 2003).

In a survey of 124 mergers Gitelson (2001) reports that firms which implemented effective communications strategies showed better results in areas such as customer focus, employee commitment and productivity than firms that delayed their communication strategy. While communication is critical throughout the M&A process in the post-acquisition phase when it becomes essential it is often mishandled. According to the psychologist Holland quoted in King (2003) 'CEOs either communicate nothing, because there are so many moving targets, or they delegate communications to two or three layers down, which ends up causing more confusion.'

Good internal communications address the personal issues such as – have I got a job?, who is my new boss? – and emotional issues such as fear, pessimism and belief in the worst case scenario. Good communications can dispel political issues such as 'hidden agendas' and rumours, and minimise politically motivated behaviours and rumour spreading. At the heart of good communications is a communication plan that addresses the information needs of the various audiences that have an interest in the M&A. The CIO's key audiences are likely to be his or her workforce, and suppliers and customers, both internal and external. The purpose of communications is not only to ensure that listeners have essential information but also to present the integration proposals in a way that they are seen to be fair, sensible and well-thought through. This can in turn help to build support for the integration plan and also to manage expectations so that stakeholders do not believe that the integration plan is going to deliver more than it is capable of.

An example of good communications is illustrated by a large US group. As soon as the deal was announced to the investors the parent company's CEO rolled out the guiding principles to the company staff worldwide. Throughout the whole integration process there were regular updates about progress. He made regular visits to all the locations for companies. The management were briefed and they kept their staff informed. There were also regular communications face to face and by email to all the working staff and after the initial period of anxiety the workforce begun to feel more comfortable about the merger because what they were hearing was backed by concrete actions so it was very much 'delivering what was preached'.

By contrast, in another acquisition that one of the author's was involved with the CEO and CIO of the acquiring company visited the newly acquired subsidiary to make a polished presentation about the acquisition and the parent company. At the end of the presentation one member of the audience got up and said: 'You have told us all the things we already knew. What we need to know is when your company is going to pay us the money that the previous owner owes us.' The team making the presentation had misunderstood the needs of the audience, the work force.

During IT integration work there is very little time to execute many tasks and communications between IT and the rest of the organisation need to be clear and concise. If one side or other does not know what is going to happen and does not, as a consequence, pull their weight the chances of IT activities being completed on time and meeting internal and external customers' expectations will be small. For IT to be successful in a M&A project those responsible for the IT organisation in the acquired company need to know whether they have a job or not, what new systems will be installed, if any, and who will be doing what. Much of this may be uncomfortable news that needs to be communicated clearly, tactfully and appropriately. An example from the interviews with CIOs demonstrates that dealing with the issue of job losses up front, in an honest and straightforward way, can be the most successful way of communicating change (see Box 6.14).

External relations

Dealing with suppliers/customers

The previous IT management issues have referred largely to internal activities. However, the external relationships that the CIO needs to manage during the integration process, particularly with customers and suppliers are equally critical. Communicating with key customers and

---

Box 6.14   IT jobs lost: open communications

In August 2002 a very successful construction, property and facilities management consultancy was split into three separate companies and put for sale.
Several bidders were interested and after a tendering period this company was
bought by its current parent company. The CIO of the acquired company noted:

> The communication process was quite open and people knew from the beginning
> where they stood. There were inevitably some people that lost their jobs. In fact half
> of the original IT staff included myself was not retained by the parent company. It
> was hard to motivate the IT staffs that were losing their jobs but despite this fact the
> IT integration process was done very professionally.

Source: extract from construction consultancy business CIO's interview.

---

suppliers should be part of the same communication system as dealing
with internal customers. The CIO needs to maintain critical customer
systems throughout the whole M&A process and keep customers
informed of the process. Negotiations with suppliers also need to insure
that changes to existing service contracts reflect the new requirements
of the enlarged group of companies. As explained in Chapter 5 new outsourcing contracts are strategic and have long-term implications so need
to be planned very carefully.

Most of the customer issues related to an M&A involve ensuring that
the correct level of service is maintained throughout the integration
work. A detailed assessment of what key customer services are affected
should be made prior to any integration work commencing. Contingency
should be built in to preserve those key customer services particularly if
the integration takes place though a busy period. In seasonal businesses,
such as retail, major IT changes should be suspended to ensure that
key systems are fully operational during Christmas. Although it is not
always possible to avoid minor disruption in an M&A IT project,
preserving the integrity of customer systems should be given top priority and the CIO should be aware of the risks to the business of not
doing so.

On the supplier side the first thing for the CIO to do is to decide
which suppliers are to be kept and which ones are no longer required.
This essential planning with associated risk management should be
done as early as possible. Where new suppliers are acquired as a result of
the M&A a normal IT management evaluation exercise should be completed using established procedures to ensure that the new supplier

meets the company quality control standards. If, as a result of the merger or acquisition transaction IT services are to be outsourced this may require a lot of attention and time by the CIO. Tendering and commercial negotiations can be lengthy.

After the merger is announced the CIO should meet with key IT suppliers and inform them about the merger and what involvement is expected from them in the integration process. Issues to be discussed include product performance, scalability, support during the transition, and service level agreements. If suppliers are to be kept a review of contracts to take account of the new size and requirements of the enlarged group is usual. Existing clauses may require changes, additional software licenses may be needed, and new price terms negotiated. If as a result of the enlarged group there is an increase in volume this may be a good time to negotiate better terms, get better service, or include the new entity in the existing contract.

If suppliers are to be discontinued the CIO needs to break the news to them carefully and look at the existing contracts, particularly the cancellation and change of control clauses to ensure that situations such as the one described in Box 6.15 are prevented. At the same time the CIO has to negotiate continuation of service and support for the necessary run-out period and insure that price escalation is avoided. If negotiations prove difficult one useful technique involves having the supplier to meet with the CEO and the CIO in the same meeting to stress the importance of reaching an agreement.

Successful external partnerships are built on regular and open communications and mutual respect. Suppliers and customers appreciate being kept informed during the merger. This can be a good opportunity to cement relationships and win support for the change.

Box 6.15   IT contract cancellation costs millions

The UK Inland Revenue could be facing a bill amounting to tens of millions (British pounds) if plans to bring together two of the largest UK government IT contracts go ahead. In order to go ahead with this plan an existing contract with Fujitsu will need to be cancelled and the supplier is demanding substantial cancellation and change payments.

The failure so far in the negotiations to terminate Fujitsu's £900 million public finance initiative contract with Customs and Excise could jeopardize the savings that the merged government agency expects to make by bringing together the two of the largest UK government contracts.

Source: Collins (2005).

Post-integration review

Review processes and learning points

The emphasis placed on planning during an M&A integration project must be complemented by firm control over the project and regular reviews of progress and achievement. Reviews not only provide the CIO and the business with assurance that the project is on track but they also provide two important opportunities. One is to communicate progress to the team and more widely to assure staff that the integration is proceeding according to plan and achieving its objectives. When the demands of integration are tough, such messages can be both encouraging and motivating. Secondly, since no plan can envisage every event or problem that may arise, regular measurement of progress against objectives allows for the plan to be adjusted to take account of the unexpected and to keep activities on track.

Good management practice by the CIO should encompass both review and learning. The M&A project, because of its intensity and inherent high risks, demands close control and constant performance review. The nature of such an integration project also requires the CIO to engage in reflective review as working with the acquired or merging company reveals features of its culture and practices and as new operations, locations and staff move under the CIO's control. The CIO needs to be open to changing his or her views and opinions from those formed during due diligence and first encounters with the new company. Finally, as the integration process draws to a conclusion the CIO needs to initiate reviews of the effectiveness of the project as a whole and in particular the processes adopted during the merger or acquisition. Such review adds to the experience bank which the CIOs involved in the research noted as highly valuable. In reality, few companies formally review mergers and acquisitions IT work but research shows that those who do learn very important points in how to avoid some of the planning and execution pitfalls.

Review is easier if the acquiring company has approached the task in a systematic way. However, the emphasis in many M&As seems to be on execution rather than planning. Experienced companies who have gone through the M&A loop a few times and learned the hard way emphasise the value of planning. With planning comes the ability to control and track the integration project and greater opportunity to learn from experience in a positive way.

Part III
Best Practice

7
The Phase Model

One of the strongest themes to emerge from the cases is the importance for IT of early involvement in the M&A process. Early involvement reduces the likelihood that IT will be expected to deliver unrealistic targets and increases the chances of valuable IT synergies being recognised when a deal is made. It also ensures that those responsible for IT are informed and prepared for the task that faces them once the M&A has been agreed. This applies as much to the acquired as the acquirer. The question then needs to be answered, how early is early in terms of useful involvement by IT in the M&A process?

The answer is not straightforward as experience shows that each acquisition is unique. However, while there may be a need to be creative and flexible when approaching a transaction this should not obviate planning. The cases discussed by the CIOs demonstrate that there are predictable outcomes as well as well-trodden paths and processes that can reduce the uncertainty and risks associated with integrating two organisations' IT systems. In fact a successful M&A integration contains a great deal of planning and requires the careful execution of a well thought through implementation strategy. Failure to complete such work in a timely or accurate fashion increases the likelihood of the M&A failing on financial or other dimensions. The approach discussed in this chapter is intended to address this area of risk by focusing on the role of IT at different stages of the M&A process.

In many respects the task facing the CIO in relation to an M&A is similar to any other major project or task. It involves the identification of aims, assembling of resources, planning, execution and review. The planning and execution of the integration of the separate IT systems involves the techniques of project management. The nature of the M&A requires attention to the processes of change management in both organisations, but particularly in the merged or acquired organisations. However, M&A is different from other management and it involves a sequence of imperatives that place particular demands on the CIO. In Part III the reader is introduced to a methodical approach to IT integration in the context of an M&A through a *Phase Model*. In the remainder of this chapter the base model is described and each of its four parts is then presented in detail in the chapters that follow.

The reader should be aware that what the phase model described below constitutes an ideal that is not always achievable. The constraints on completing fully every stage of the model occur as a result of tight deadlines, secrecy, organisational and political sensitivities, and limited resources. The CIO needs to complete as much of each stage as possible and be aware of those areas where estimates and assumptions replace accurate information and fact. He or she should also be clear about how much of the integration has been planned and how much has been left to chance. However, there are some essentials that the CIO should strive to complete, even in the most adverse of circumstances and these are indicated in relation to each part of the model.

The phase model

The idea of the model is to provide a practical guide for anyone contemplating an IT M&A project. It aims both to provide a guide or road map for the CIO faced with such a project and to highlight best practices used by M&A's specialists, consultants and CIOs with a successful track record in this area. The model is presented as an aid to those involved in the IT side of an M&A, but it could be adapted to other functional areas. As a model it should also be of interest to senior executives or board members who want to understand better the role played by IT during the M&A process.

The four elements of the phase model are:

Figure 7.1   The phase model: key elements

Each of these elements has a distinctive set of aims, with associated activities, and deliverables.

Figure 7.2 The phase model: elements aims

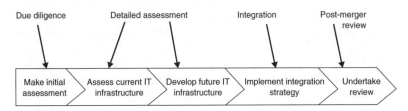

Figure 7.3 The phase model: key activities

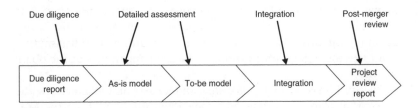

Figure 7.4 The phase model: key deliverables

Each element also involves IT in particular way. The phase model methodology follows a typical project structure

Figure 7.5 The phase model: project methodology

Due diligence is a stage that is unique to M&As as opposed to other organisational and management change projects. In the due diligence stage the focus is on gaining an understanding as quickly as possible about the state of the target company's IT systems infrastructure. The activities are to do with understanding and anticipating the synergies and potential difficulties that may arise during integration. The key deliverable from this phase is the due diligence report which represents a high level assessment of the challenges and opportunities ahead. Due diligence is a phase where the CIO is not always involved but one where it is essential for the CIO to be involved if the benefits of M&A are to be realised in relation to the IT function.

The second phase called *detailed assessment* does not normally begin until the M&A deal has been negotiated. The aim of this phase is to work out in as much detail as possible the integration roadmap. The key activities revolve around, first of all, understanding and describing the current (As-Is)operating model; secondly, working out what the new (To-Be) operating model should be; and thirdly, identifying the gap between the two scenarios so that the details can be worked out for how to get from one to the other. At the end of the phase the key deliverable is the integration strategy and migration plan that should be tailored to achieving the objectives of the M&A. The CIO must take a lead during this phase but will need to involve a wider planning team drawn from both organisations involved in the transaction. The detailed assessment phase is not just purely about planning but is also about the opportunity to build the team's morale and enthusiasm that will carry the organisations through the implementation of the phase to follow.

The third phase is about *integration* and focuses on implementing the integration plan. The key activities are about migrating from the As-Is model to the To-Be model, with particular emphasis on speed of execution and the attainment of quick wins. Quick wins are those post-integration IT activities that are easy to implement and at the same time provide visible and tangible benefits. Quick wins are seen as key success factors in delivering the synergies identified in the two previous phases. Their function is also to generate goodwill and commitment to undertaking longer-term and more complex and difficult integration activities. The deliverables from this phase extend over a period of time starting with quick wins and ending when the IT systems in the two companies are fully integrated and are operating at pre-M&A capacity. As in the previous phase, the CIO must take a leading role in integration. In this phase it is likely that everyone involved in IT will be engaged in the process to a greater or lesser extent.

The fourth and final phase is that of *post-merger review*. The aim of this phase is to learn from the experience of the M&A. This phase should be a natural process for a learning organisation, but it is often either missed out or completed in a cursory fashion. The activities involved include taking stock of the results achieved, evaluating the way the IT function approached the task and building a set of best practices for future M&As. The deliverable from this phase is a post-merger assessment report. The CIO may not be the person undertaking this activity but should ensure that it is done and should take a personal interest in the findings and should champion improvements based on the learning that has occurred.

Each phase can be estimated to take a number of weeks, or months, to complete. The time involved will depend upon the scale and complexity of the tasks and the time scales set for the M&A. As will be discussed later, such timescales are always negotiable to some degree and it is the role of the CIO to ensure that the timescales agreed are realistic and achievable. The timescales in Figure 7.6 are indicative. The most variable phase is the integration phase that, dependent upon the approach taken, can last from a few weeks to years. The review phase should always be short; due diligence is also usually confined within a few

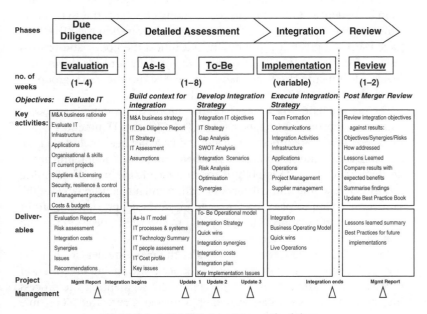

Figure 7.6   M&A IT integration methodology

weeks. As is also suggested on the diagram the CIO will want to identify key progress review points throughout the M&A to ensure that the project is on track.

The phase model identifies the four stages as distinctive sets of tasks and processes. In an ideal world they would all be carried out sequentially and in order. However, as the cases illustrate, the four stages may be truncated to three, two or even one. Also some of the stages may be carried out concurrently. Such a way of proceeding can be the result of poor awareness of what is involved in an M&A or the difficulties imposed by the transaction itself or the environment.

The first and fourth stages of the model are not always executed. Companies that fail to do this are usually displaying a lack of understanding and appreciation of what is involved in an M&A, and thereby take very considerable risks. Companies risk stepping into the unknown by failing to undertake effective due diligence. Examples of unwelcome surprises include poor IT infrastructure, inflexible agreements with suppliers, undocumented systems and a poorly skilled IT workforce. Examples of difficulties that are better discovered earlier than later include incompatible systems and high running costs. Companies that fail to undertake a post-merger review miss the opportunity to learn from experience and also cannot demonstrate that the synergistic benefits have been achieved. The individuals involved in the M&A may have learned a great deal personally, but unless the policy and process lessons for the company are drawn out formally and set down in a review document, they are liable to be lost to the next group of managers involved in such transactions.

The second and third stages of the model may sometimes occur concurrently. This may happen where the CIO and IT function is not involved in the M&A process until late and have not been included in the due diligence. Another scenario is when companies adopt unrealistic deadlines and the CIO is obliged to short-circuit the normal planning processes by moving immediately into action and integration while at the same time trying to plan the longer term. Rushing and running out of time in a poorly planned M&A can lead to short-term decision-making that companies regret later.

For the CIO awareness of the stages of the phase model can provide several benefits. The environment produced within an organisation involved in an M&A is one of uncertainty. By segmenting the process into distinct phases with associated objectives and tasks the CIO is able to bring more structure into the process, thereby reducing uncertainty. Structure can save time and costs as well as anxiety and help to reduce the risks involved in the M&A process. An approach such as the phase model can also provide a common framework within which the two companies or organisations involved in the transaction can work and assist them to develop communications based on identified aims and tasks. Thirdly, by identifying key roles, activities and tasks it is easier to research and identify best practice and to train and develop staff to undertake M&A work more effectively.

The larger and more complex the M&A, the more formal and detailed the structures and planning that are needed to tackle the task involved in delivering successful outcomes. A very large transaction will require multiple analyses, plans and projects for completion; they can all, however, ultimately be fitted into the four key phases identified above. It should be noted that while the phase model may appear, diagrammatically, as a set of independent steps, in reality it is a highly integrated process from start to finish. As a result of this interdependence over time the CIO cannot afford to enter the process late: time and again the literature and the cases cited confirm that the earlier the CIO becomes actively involved in the process and planning commences, the greater the chances of success. Finally, as is clear from the different cases discussed, all M&A's have elements in common, yet all are different. The phase model can provide a guide but at the end of the day every CIO should use it in a way that is sensible and appropriate for the circumstances involved.

In the succeeding chapters each of the four phases is examined in greater detail. This includes identifying the variety of tasks and activities that may take place within each phase as well as presenting tools and techniques that may prove useful.

8
Due Diligence

Before a company decides to acquire or merge with another a process of 'due diligence' is undertaken. The term due diligence applies to the investigation and evaluation performed by the acquiring company into the company to be acquired. In this process, often carried out by M&A's consultancy firms on behalf of the buyer, a general examination of the target company's assets, liabilities and capabilities is undertaken. The objectives of the due diligence typically are:

- To identify points that have an impact on the value of the target company and therefore affect price and bid negotiations.
- To reduce the risk involved in a deal, for example, by obtaining warranties against legal claims.
- To understand the potential synergies between the companies and gauge whether or not these are achievable.

From the IT perspective, the focus of the due diligence phase should be to gain an understanding as quickly as possible about the state of the target company IT systems infrastructure. The activities involved will be to do with understanding the integration difficulties and costs. The key deliverable from this phase is the due diligence report that represents a high level assessment of the challenges and opportunities ahead.

Involving IT in due diligence

According to KPMG (2000) the intrinsic value that underlies future profitability of the business on a standalone basis often accounts for 90 per cent of the pre-deal valuation and therefore a lot of the emphasis in the due diligence phase is concentrated on the financial aspects of the business. In the same study it is also noted that strategy and synergy account for 50 per cent of this value. In terms of synergies, IT accounts for a growing part of this intrinsic value, possibly as much as 20 per cent or more in some deals and it is therefore one of the reasons why IT, should not be omitted from the due diligence phase.

Lees (2003) notes that despite poor knowledge by the acquirer of the operation of the target firm accounting for a large proportion of the difficulties encountered in implementing a M&A, due diligence has only slowly expanded beyond financial, legal and commercial concerns. Given the centrality of IT to modern businesses, there are strong arguments for ensuring that it is considered at the earliest stages of contemplating M&A. A lack of a clear M&A strategy and the role of IT within it is sometimes the reason why IT is not involved explicitly in due diligence. Conversely, the involvement of IT at the beginning of the M&A process is eased if the acquiring company already has an IT strategy and has considered the impact of new acquisitions within it. Ideally the CIO or IT Manager should be involved as part of the acquisition team. If no CIO or qualified IT person is available the alternative is to use external IT consultants to advise but, most importantly, *do not ignore IT*. Many companies have paid the price by making unrealistic assumptions about IT synergies or costs that later proved inaccurate, thus making costly mistakes.

The IT task in due diligence

The key IT objective of the due diligence phase is to understand the target company's infrastructure (people, process and technology). Due diligence allows the buyer to make an assessment of the target firm's capabilities, potential integration problems, costs, and synergies based on their own IT strategy and that of the new parent company. As indicated above, before starting this exercise it is essential to have a clear view of the business strategy and rationale for the acquisition or merger.

The endpoint of the exercise is to feed back the results of the IT due diligence to the M&A team. To achieve this there are a number of activities and tasks that the CIO, or person responsible for IT, needs to plan and undertake. An overview of the main activities for this phase is shown in Figure 8.1.

The first task is to plan the due diligence thoroughly using detailed templates or checklists from previous M&A experience. If there is no relevant previous experience or the company has no senior IT person consideration should be given to using external consultants. However, some companies prefer the in-house route only. In deciding how to evaluate IT during due

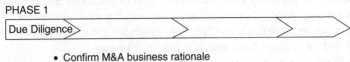

Due Diligence should start before the deal is completed...

PHASE 1

Due Diligence

Key Activities

- Confirm M&A business rationale
- Evaluate IT infrastructure, applications, IT organisation and skills
- Identify current IT projects
- Understand suppliers' contracts and licensing
- Assess security, resilience and control
- Assess IT management practices
- Identify costs and budgets

... to ensure you understand your target company's IT strengths and weaknesses

Figure 8.1   Due diligence phase: activity overview

diligence and beyond it is important to remember that M&A IT projects are not conventional IT projects and require particularly high levels of planning, analytical and execution skills not always found in conventional IT departments.

Due diligence is about the early identification of the risks. Having a robust and structured process that methodically reviews all the key risks – technical, financial, people – can avoid embarrassing situations, particularly involving difficult transactions, where parties have their own hidden agendas and the information released may be suspect. Formality can also make unwanted or unwelcome advances more acceptable and less confrontational.

The starting point, as with any other strategic project is to understand the overall strategy and rationale for the merger. This enables the IT activities to be focused and based on specific strategic objectives. For example, in one recent IT M&A due diligence, the acquiring company had already decided that IT integration was not an objective and that the acquired company would continue to use their current systems. However, this did not mean that IT considerations played no part in due diligence. What the acquiring company was most interested in getting out of the IT due diligence was the answer to two key questions. The first question was about risk: was it safe for the acquiring company to allow the acquired company to link into the existing corporate network? The second question was about control: could the acquired company's current systems produce monthly reports to satisfy the information requirements of the new owners?

However, although the acquiring company may have been watching potential M&A targets for some time, due diligence is invariably a short and focused process. Depending on the size and complexity of the transaction this phase may typically take up to 4 weeks within which a considerable amount of data needs to be collected and evaluated. Data collection should be ideally done by more than one person so that cross checking and validation of information is possible. During due diligence the key IT activity is the detailed gathering of internal information to assess current IT infrastructure, applications, processes and people. A typical information-gathering checklist is shown in Box 8.1.

To achieve the aims of due diligence it is essential to have a well defined data collection strategy. Typical challenges of due diligence include the amount of information available, the short time to collect it and the validation process thereafter. Collecting information before the merger is announced can be difficult particularly if the target company sees the approach as unfriendly. An opposite problem can be the sheer volume of data involved, particularly in a large and complex transaction. The short time span involved means that only the most relevant and targeted data should be collected. Due diligence must not be conducted as open-ended research. Effective data collection for these purposes implies using as detailed process as possible and making use of any existing and externally collected information such as that provided by external auditors. The question of confidentiality and secrecy is clearly very important. Yet, information can still be gathered through external or

---

Box 8.1   Due diligence: typical set of information collected

- Number of operating units involved in the transaction
- Overview of business operations and IT operations
- Number of IS staff, their skills, organisation and management practices
- Number and type of IT applications
- Current key committed projects
- IT infrastructure and technical environment details such as:
  - Technology and architecture
  - Number and type of hardware used
  - Network capacity (bandwidth)
  - Locations
  - Number of users
- Annual budgets (capital and revenue)
- Key suppliers and contracts
- Published IT strategies and plans

third party sources. If the acquisition or merger is of a friendly nature this exercise is, of course, much easier.

While the scale and complexity of information to be gathered regarding a large and complex transaction can appear daunting, it is important also not underestimate small acquisitions They often pose extremely interesting challenges that require innovative thinking. It is certainly the case that the amount of work and management time should not be underestimated and they demand a similar approach to that used in larger transactions. Whatever the scale of the M&A, the first chance to get it right is at due diligence stage; later is much more difficult.

The collection of the above information gives the consultant or the CIO the first indication of how well the current IT organisation in the target company is performing. Understanding key projects is also valuable, as it shows how recently or otherwise the company has invested in IT. Small companies or companies that have decided to put themselves for sale are often negligent in investing. Indeed this is often one of the reasons for the M&A in the first place. In this case lack of investment in IT is not unusual. Their systems are often kept precariously afloat by relying on one single person who has been with the company a long time and he or she is the only one that knows how the system works. Although involving small transactions, such scenarios can imply high levels of risk.

In a different scenario, a company might be approached unexpectedly by an unwanted bidder while they are in the middle of a big system implementation. In a case that one of the authors was involved with, the eventually acquired company had spent several million dollars in implementing an ERP system which at the time that the merger was announced they were half-way through implementing. During the due diligence it emerged that the new ERP had not been accepted by some of the countries involved. The possibility of a new company buying them was seen as an opportunity to stop the ERP implementation in their countries. Deciding to cancel the project or continue was not only a critical economic decision but it also took on a high political significance.

Another key activity of this phase should be the assessment of security risks. As more companies trade externally with business partners the risks associated with network access and control becomes prominent. In a retail company that bought a company with several hundred stores, addressing this risk meant upgrading their point of sale terminals and server hardware through significant investment.

Assessing the people and existing IT organisation is a key element of due diligence. This is never a science, more of an art, and requires a lot of experience and interpersonal skills. In a small company this may be a simple task. In larger mergers this may be one of the most difficult and time consuming activities. In a 'merger of equals' with two large IT departments, each with a considerable powerbase, understanding the management processes and practices would be essential because the success of the future strategy will be dependent on whose systems and management are recommended during the merger.

Due diligence involves collecting data and information related to finding out the cost profile of the company to be acquired. Particular emphasis should be placed on understanding the current spend versus that of the acquiring company. To avoid political arguments it is often the case that companies use external consultants when objective advice is sought. Consultants use industry best practices to benchmark cost profiles. A more difficult task is to asses the value provided by IT. Because of the short time of the engagement a statement from senior management or key users tend to provide a preliminary evaluation which should be checked more thoroughly during the detailed assessment.

Finally, due diligence activity involves collection of external information regarding key customers and suppliers including their product, services, and contractual terms. This area is often overlooked and companies find that their expectations for synergies are sometimes over optimistic because they neglected to go into the 'small print' of existing suppliers' contracts and cannot terminate long-term contractual obligations with existing suppliers without heavy penalties. An example of this was the case of a European energy company that, having set its eyes on a foreign acquisition, was forced to withdraw its offer when, during the due diligence, it emerged that the IT synergies that were planned were not possible because the target company had a long standing contract with one of the suppliers for the outsourcing of their data-centre facilities.

With international transactions becoming more common, overcoming international cultural differences is a key success factor in getting the M&A right. Commentators such as Angwin (2001) have noted that due diligence is particularly complex in cross-border M&As. Part of the complexity stems from the difficulties in evaluating intangibles and the softer aspects of organisations. For example, getting management practices right in a cross-border situation avoids the risks of extending the integration time and making change management more complex. However, it is not easy, within a due diligence investigation to gauge how easy or difficult such cross-border alignment of management practices will be. In the IT field attention must also be paid to the legal and commercial environment in which target company operates: for example labour laws may make potential re-structuring of IT operations very expensive; suppliers may not support sales in some countries making single-sourcing difficult; or taxation may be favourable or unfavourable to IT investment.

The information described above is collected by a variety of written and oral sources and by means of interviews or workshops. The role of external consultants can be useful in this phase because it reduces the risk of leaving out something important (first-time companies involved in the M&A process are particularly vulnerable), the operation is completed in a short space of time and more importantly they can offer objective and professional advice to both companies.

Deliverables

The key deliverable of this phase is typically a written evaluation report with a high level risk assessment highlighting key issues and the potential impact for the integration process, costs and benefits and a list of recommendations with all the key points. An example of the contents of a typical due diligence IT report would include all the following headings (see Box 8.2).

Limited time, and the context in which due diligence is undertaken, mean that the data and information collected will in certain aspects be incomplete and may be less reliable or valid than is desirable. For this reason it is essential to document the assumptions that are made in coming

---

Box 8.2   Due diligence report: typical headings

- Introduction
- Management summary
- IT infrastructure
- Application architecture
- Hardware and software
- Organisation and skills
- Development approach and current developments
- Supplier relationships and contracts
- Security, resilience and control
- IT Cost and budgets
- Risk assessment
- Integration costs
- Potential synergies (depending on the scope, sometimes this is left out)
- Key integration issues, likely timescales
- Key findings and recommendations

to conclusions within the due diligence report. The report should also explain the business assumptions made and their implications for IT. Such assumptions underlie decisions on costs, resources, and implementation strategy and should always be made explicit. The value of the due diligence process is that any assumptions made at the M&A bidding stage about potential IT synergies or IT issues will be supported by a detailed preliminary assessment. Confirming the IT capabilities or otherwise of the target company should provide management with a good feel about what is possible in this important area.

9
Detailed Assessment

Introduction

The structured approach presented in Chapter 8 started with the due diligence of IT before the merger is announced. This is a snapshot of the new company's IT organization, processes and systems. Armed with this information both IT and business management are in position to make rational forecasts and apply judgment about the 'intrinsic' value of the new company's IT systems.

Detailed assessment is the next key requirement before full integration is contemplated. This detailed assessment exposes the target company to searching questions which confirm or deny the assumptions made about their IT systems during the due diligence phase. It also confirms and details the expected synergies and implementation issues.

In the detailed assessment phase the focus is on working out the integration road map in as much detail as possible. The key activities are firstly, understanding and describing the current operating model; secondly, working out what the new, post-merger/acquisition operating model should be; thirdly, identifying the gap between the two scenarios; and finally working out the details of how to get there. At the end of this phase the key deliverable is the integration strategy and migration plan.

This phase starts when the merger has been approved, sometimes earlier, depending on whether or not due diligence was done. Ideally when the detailed assessment is started the objectives of the M&A are known and have been communicated by the CEO and the Board. Unfortunately, this is not always the case and detailed assessment may have to begin in an atmosphere of partial knowledge and uncertainty. This is particularly true in cases where there has been a hostile M&A bid. In this situation the CIO's prior knowledge about the transaction may have been limited. The

CIO will also be working within a set of constraints relating to time, money and resources that have been set by the basic terms of the M&A deal and decisions already taken about what the transaction is required to deliver to the company.

Developing the integration strategy is divided into two logical steps. The first step, called here the As-Is Model, analyses and reviews the current situation before integration starts. The second step, the To-Be Model, explores the possible IT organisation and processes that could exist after integration of the separate companies or organisations. The interaction and ultimate fusion of the two models informs the implementation strategy. In practice these two steps are not always executed in a sequential fashion. Those charged with the detailed assessment will move from a focus on As-Is at the beginning of the process to one of To-Be at the end of the process. Throughout this phase there has to be a dialogue between the two models. However, it is important to recognise that each step has its own requirements and approach. The first step is about identifying the context in which the M&A is to take place, for example the markets in which the acquired company is operating. The second step is about identifying and deciding what the newly merged or acquired organisation will look like, how this can be achieved, and the changes needed in the parent organisation to accommodate them.

The As-Is model

The precise length of time needed to complete this stage will depend on the scale and complexity of the M&A and the staff resources available to undertake the work. It will also depend on whether or not due diligence was done. The CIO should allow several weeks for the detailed assessment phase to be completed. The dictates of the M&A timetable will normally mean that the longest this phase can last is 3 months. The larger and more complex the transaction, the bigger the team that will be needed to undertake the research required in this phase. If the problems, the timescales and the available resources do not fit, the CIO, together with the mergers and acquisition team and other senior managers, must take a strategic decision about limiting the scope of the initial integration objectives. The implementation plan should never exceed in scope the information and data upon which it is based: proposals should be realistic, supported by evidence and best estimates rather than hunches and guesses.

An overview with the main activities for the first step of this phase is shown in Figure 9.1.

Detailed assessment should start after due diligence is done...

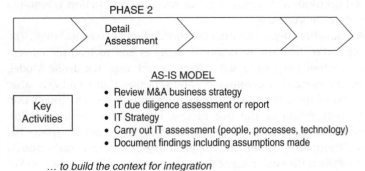

Figure 9.1   Detailed assessment phase: activity overview (As-Is model)

To undertake this phase successfully requires a team approach. The selection and formation of the initial integration team should take place at the beginning of the detailed assessment phase. Sometimes this team is the same as the one involved during the due diligence stage and sometimes it is not. If due diligence was undertaken by consultants this may be the first point at which internal staff are involved in the change process. Depending on the size and complexity of the M&A operation a number of people drawn from the parent and the subsidiary companies, will be needed. In some cases external consultants will also be needed to provide specific expertise, fill gaps and to provide an independent third party viewpoint in difficult situations.

The structuring of the team that undertakes the detailed assessment phase is in itself important. The team must contain both technical expertise and analytical capability and ideally previous M&A experience to take into account organisational and political considerations. The composition will also reflect an acquiring company's approach to integration by being more or less inclusive. Political balance is important in mergers, particularly where they are presented as being a 'merger of equals'. A well-constructed team that reflects the realities of the integration that is going to occur can provide an accurate assessment and develop more realistic plans than one which lacks skills, knowledge or clout. It is essential to be aware of private agendas in the integration process. Moving from the current to a future operating model requires careful selection of people, systems and locations. To be successful one needs to circumvent (as much

as is possible) private agendas of key stakeholders and be prepared to negotiate flexible options. The involvement of the CIO as part of the M&A integration team is a pre-requisite for achieving realistic IT synergies and a
successful and effective IT integration.

The starting point for this phase is to confirm the strategic objectives
for the merger and specifically how they relate to IT. This is particularly
important if the due diligence was not done and this is the first time that
an IT assessment is being made. As we saw in the due diligence phase,
this starting point confirms the strategic thinking for the merger.
However, even if due diligence was done, some aspects may have
changed since it was carried out, and this confirmatory activity is still
required to give focus to the IT work to be carried out. Sometimes there
is a long gap between the merger being announced and integration actually starting, typically when regulatory permission is needed by the
European or US Monopoly Commissions.

If no previous due diligence has been carried out then an overview of the
new company's IT capabilities, weaknesses and risks is required. This heli-
copter view, normally provided by the due diligence assessment report is
needed before starting the detailed work. This is an important document
because it will also give an indication whether or not there are likely to be
any synergies and also what the main costs and risks will be. A strategic
overview approach guides and gives focus to the integration efforts.

A key activity during the latter part of the detailed assessment phase
will be to decide on the future IT strategy for the merged organisations.
Understanding both the current and previously planned IT strategy in
the acquired company, and in the acquiring one, in the earlier stages of
assessment will help to identify gaps and what needs to be done to fill
them in the second step. Assessment should look at strategies for both
technology and people, particularly if the objective is not to retain
groups of staff after the merger.

The bulk of activities in this first step revolve around understanding
the current operating model. These are normally broken down by the
relevant functional or technology area, for example development, operations, networking and call centre; and by applications and processes.
Typical questions addressed by this phase are shown in Box 9.1.

Note: if no due diligence report exists then the initial set of questions
as indicated in chapter 8 apply before the detailed work can commence.
In practice the due diligence questions on basic infrastructure are added
to the list on Box 9.1.

To gather the information needed to answer these questions standard checklists or templates may be used as they were during due diligence for data

---

Box 9.1   Typical questions addressed (1)

1. What IT synergies have been identified among the two companies?
2. How do they compare with assumptions made at pre-merger state?
3. What changes are needed to achieve them? Where? Why?
4. What are the risks?
5. What are the benefits? What are the quick wins?
6. What are the costs? Are they affordable? (i.e. do we want to spend this money?)
7. What are the IT implications for both companies in terms of change?
8. What are the IT strategy options for implementation?
9. What are the options available? What is the criterion used to choosing between them? Strategy, technology, people, process, costs, benefits, risks, constraints, assumptions, top management view?
10. As a result of the above what specific actions or steps do we need take?

---

recording and for communications within the integration team. The sources of data and information to be able to answer the questions posed in Box 9.1 may include existing documents and data and interviews. Given the limited time available, information requirements should be carefully specified and identified before the gathering of data and documents takes place. As data collection proceeds, the team undertaking the detailed assessment needs to document its findings on the current operating model including the assumptions being made on process, technology and costs. This documentation will form the evidence that supports the strategic decisions that are made about IT in the merged organisation and integration strategy and plan.

The deliverable from step one is the baseline operating model with the answers to the questions identified mentioned earlier in this chapter (see Box 9.1). This is a formal assessment of where the merged or acquired company is [the As-Is-model] before the integration strategy is decided upon. A typical assessment report produced at this stage would cover the same type of headings as shown in the due diligence chapter (see Box 8.2) but in greater detail to reflect a more extensive analysis. For example, at the due diligence stage the quantification of synergies would have been broad estimates because of the limited time and information available. On the other hand during the detailed assessment the level of information and the amount of time would normally allow for these estimates to be validated and refined. The typical headings for a report after the detailed assessment has been completed are shown in Box 9.2. The contents of the report may be presented on their own or more likely to be combined with the work in step two as the basis for the analysis and recommendations of the entire detailed assessment phase.

Detailed assessment should start after due diligence is done...

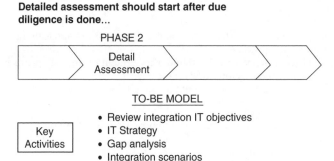

... *to develop the integration strategy*

Figure 9.2 Detailed assessment phase: activity overview (To-Be model)

The To-Be model

The second step in the detailed assessment phase is to develop the future operating IT model (To-Be model). The key activities involved are shown in Figure 9.2.

The framework for the To-Be model

The CIO does not have the freedom to develop whatever future operating model he or she would prefer. The To-Be model will be limited by sets of constraints that need to be clearly identified at the beginning of the integration strategy building process. The first set of constraints are the facts and figures which have been identified in the As-Is model. Where the model is incomplete assumptions have to be made and clearly noted. The second set of constraints is located in the terms of the M&A itself and the objectives set by the parent company for the outcome of the transactions. These constraints may include timescales for integration, costs savings, performance targets and operating requirements. The extent to which these constraints are fixed or negotiable will vary and may change as the implications of prior decisions are made clear through the detailed assessment phase. The third set of constraints relates to policies and expectations about the ways that the integration is conducted. The most fundamental of these is the approach to be taken to integration. Some companies have more or less fixed policies on how integration should be handled; others do not and the CIO has to factor the choice of approach into the generation of one or more To-Be models.

Box 9.2   Assessment report: typical headings

- Current processes and systems. This should cover main IT applications and key business processes
- Current IT technology used. This should cover main technology platforms, degree of obsolescene, supporting arrangements, etc.
- Current IT organization. This should include:
    - people skills and experience
    - management practices
    - the role of IT in the organization and how is meeting business expectations
- Current cost profile
- Key issues facing the IT organization in terms of:
    - people
    - processes
    - technology
    - cultural
    - political

Approaches to integration

In developing the 'To-Be' model a number of different approaches can be taken to integration. The choice of approach will depend not only on the strategic objectives of the M&A, but also the acquiring company's attitude and philosophy towards standardisation, centralisation and other systems factors. In general the approaches adopted towards integration can be categorised as follows.

- little or no integration,
- total integration,
- a mixture of the two (sometimes intended to be 'best of both worlds').

In certain situations the parent company takes a 'leave alone' approach to its acquisition and seeks little or no integration of business processes and IT systems. This option, where applicable, is simple and straightforward; not much change, things are left as before. An example of this pattern of integration involved a retail company where the strategic thrust of the acquisition was to enter a new market and gain market share. In this context the parent company was not interested in changing any of the IT systems. Other examples include Sony acquiring Columbia Pictures and Mannersmann and Westinghouse/CBS (Roberts 2004).

The total integration approach is also common. For US multinationals this is frequently the preferred solution and it is becoming common with other nationalities too. Total integration means that the acquired company moves to use its parent company's business systems (rarely the other way around). The change involved is significant but limited to the acquired company. This option is also normally straightforward from a technical viewpoint. However, there are exceptions such as we saw in C3. Here, the parent company decided to try new technology in the new subsidiary, of which it had no previous experience, with the view of then using it group-wide. In this case the risks associated with implementing new technology should be carefully evaluated (see Chapter 5).

If the acquired company is much smaller than the parent company the integration effort can be less difficult than if the acquired company is of the same size or bigger than the parent company. The total integration approach opens up implementation issues regarding people and power, and can engender 'turf wars'. The bigger and stronger the merged or acquired company is relative to the acquirer, the greater these problems are likely to be. Whoever is in charge of the integration plan must be aware of and successfully deal with such issues. To succeed with a total integration approach there should ideally be experience of a successful previous M&A of this type, strong change management and leadership, and a ready made IT solution from the buying company that is feasible for the acquired company.

The most complicated and risky option is to go for a mixture of systems. This means both companies' systems have to change and the transition period is likely to be more complex and longer with an increasing chance of delays. This approach makes very significant demands on both organisations and requires an unusual degree of clarity of vision, strong leadership and management commitment. The degree and extent of change involved, because it affects both companies, increases the risk of failure so this option, when taken, should be chosen with full understanding of the risks involved. An example of this from one of the authors' experience involved two companies in the distribution area. The parent company wanted to standardise on SAP but the acquired company had a well developed in-house system which it wanted to retain. After considerable discussion and negotiation the final solution was to implement a mixture of the two systems. Inevitably this approach took a long time to integrate. As a result what appeared to be a way to get the 'best of both worlds' in reality was not very successful because of the additional time and costs required. In fact the two IT organisations were still arguing two years after the merger as to whether they should have gone for a single solution. Unfortunately, in this case, the politics of the merger were too powerful to allow a simpler and more effective solution at the time.

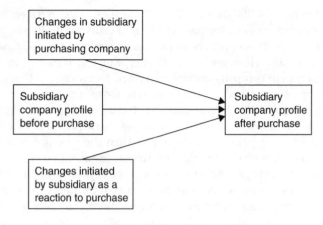

Source: based on Child *et al.* 2003.

Figure 9.3   Post-acquisition change process

The pattern of change that eventually emerges is normally a consequence of the change process that takes place in the post acquisition phase. This can be mapped graphically, see Figure 9.3.

Change can also be shown by a simple diagram that illustrates the amount of change and hence risks that any of the companies will undertake depending on the option chosen. Assuming that Company A is the Parent Company and Company B is the subsidiary option 1 leaves both companies with little or no change. This is a low risk-low reward option (in terms of synergies). Option 2 assumes that Parent company introduces its IT systems into its acquired subsidiary. This would be a low risk-high reward option and the one that is most frequently adopted in M&As. The opposite occurs in Option 3. In this case it is the parent company that adopts the systems from the subsidiary. The risks, however, may be rather greater than in Option 2, particularly if the parent company's size is large. Option 4 is a high risk–high reward strategy. It can emerge by default in situations where there is no clear IT strategy. It can also be adopted as a deliberate strategy towards a merger of equals where the merged companies have the potential for achieving far more as a joint entity. However, as indicated previously, the risks associated with this strategy can be very high. The terms suggest that the two companies are equal and share the new organisation in equal terms. This is almost never the case: even if advertised as a merger of equals there is always one partner that is more dominant. Options 1 and 2 are much more common than 3 and 4.

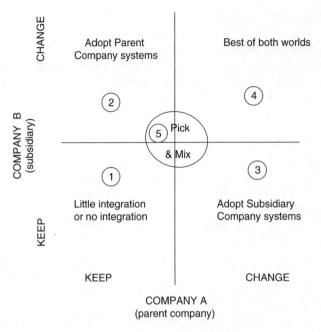

Source: Adapted from J. Glyde *et al.* (2003).

Figure 9.4   Strategic options: IT systems

The 'pick and mix' approach (option 5) indicated by the circle in the centre of the diagram (see Figure 9.4) should be avoided in almost all circumstances because mixing solutions is rarely easy and invariably takes longer than originally thought.

Gap analysis

A key activity in the development of the To-Be model is to review the current IT operating model against the M&A's strategic objectives and to determine the gap between the two. This analysis process will highlight where gaps and opportunities for synergies exist. It will also indicate the cost and complexity of the integration task. As a result specific options can be developed. For instance, if the M&A objective is to leverage all the possible synergies among the two companies, then the IT emphasis should be on making the necessary IT cost and process improvements. In this scenario the analysis of current IT costs will be paramount. This analysis is usually done either by comparing the acquired company's costs against parent company's own figures or to benchmark against leaders in the company's own industry.

On the other hand a different case would be that of a company that is acquired by its new parent company for the purpose of obtaining new products or technology. In this situation the IT integration strategy may well be to leave the new subsidiary's systems untouched and for the parent company to provide more IT resources and IT capabilities to the subsidiary (e.g. larger network, more powerful computing facilities, access to parent company's suppliers or a combination of all three).

In reality the relationship between the use of technology and the financial case is always difficult to separate and decisions made on one affect the other and vice versa. It is for this reason that the CIO should analyse them carefully before committing to a particular strategy. Before deciding on a particular strategy the CIO needs to assess the gap that exists between current and future position. To decide this aspect the CIO must consider the following questions (see Box 9.3).

Once all the elements of the gap analysis have been collected and analysed the team is in a position to develop the integration strategy. This is an iterative process and typically lasts 3 to 4 weeks. Before submitting the final recommendations it is always a good idea to discuss them with the business sponsor and other key stakeholders that are not part of the team to gain their support and receive feedback. In this way problems can be anticipated and surprises eliminated before the final choices are made.

A successful integration strategy is a combination of thorough analysis and pragmatic implementation. It needs to consider the practical aspects such as cultural setting, organisational context (e.g. political positioning), management leadership, quick wins, right amount and quality of implementation resources, and project management.

Box 9.3 Gap analysis: typical questions

1. Which current systems are to be changed and which ones are to remain?
2. Which new systems are put in?
3. What are the priorities and areas for integration?
4. What IT resources from the acquired company are to be kept or let go?
5. What technologies and standards are to be used?
6. What is the role of IT in the new business environment?
7. What are the IT synergies?
8. What are the integration costs?
9. What is the new organization model?
10. What are the main integration scenarios and their advantages/ disadvantages?

Techniques for developing the To-Be model

Much of the preliminary work on the As-Is model will be descriptive. However, in order to move towards the second, To-Be model, the integration team needs to analyse the picture of the acquired or merged operation that is emerging. The CIO can draw on a number of established techniques that can be useful in such analysis and in presentation of the topics to other senior managers and the board. By analysing the facts and figures that have been obtained, and bringing broader contextual information to bear on the matter, analytical tools can help in obtaining answers to the strategic questions posed and to generate strategic options for the To-Be model. The following techniques are offered as illustrations. The decision to use them or not is dependent on the specific situation encountered to which they can be applied. They should be considered as an aid rather than as a prescription. Not every integration team will want to use all of them. The selection of tools will depend on the circumstances of the particular merger of acquisition.

SWOT analysis

An important aspect of the IT assessment phase is to consider how the combined IT organisations would look like into the future. From an internal customer view point it is important to consider what would be the capabilities and resources of the combined IT organisation (*strengths*). For example, the ability to provide internal expertise in certain new or existing technologies may eliminate the need to buy those skills externally. Similarly, the assessment should also consider which aspects of the new IT organisation are likely to create problems (*weaknesses*). For example, as a result of the merger certain essential skills may be lost and this may impair the ability of the new IT department to provide an adequate level of service.

From an external customer view point the assessment needs to consider also the potential benefit areas (*opportunities*) created as a result of the two companies combining capabilities and resources. For example, the ability to combine purchasing power could provide higher leverage with current or new suppliers. Likewise, the potential risks or *threats* need to be assessed. For example, the ability to restructure or outsource certain type of services in certain countries may require more time and effort than expected due to labour legislation in the countries concerned.

SWOT (strengths, weaknesses, opportunities and threats) analysis is a simple and yet very useful and popular technique to be able to represent the above in a diagrammatic form. The chart is divided into four quadrants. In the top left quadrant the key strengths for the combined

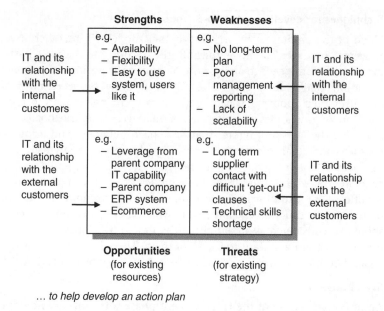

	Strengths	**Weaknesses**	
IT and its relationship with the internal customers	e.g. – Availability – Flexibility – Easy to use system, users like it	e.g. – No long-term plan – Poor management reporting – Lack of scalability	IT and its relationship with the internal customers
IT and its relationship with the external customers	e.g. – Leverage from parent company IT capability – Parent company ERP system – Ecommerce	e.g. – Long term supplier contact with difficult 'get-out' clauses – Technical skills shortage	IT and its relationship with the external customers
	Opportunities (for existing resources)	**Threats** (for existing strategy)	

... to help develop an action plan

Figure 9.5   SWOT analysis: example

IT department and its relationship with the internal customers are identified. In the top right quadrant we do the same for the weaknesses. The bottom left quadrant identifies the potential opportunities for existing resources. The bottom right quadrant identifies the potential threats for the existing IT strategy. The decision on what to include is clearly dependent in each M&A transaction. The objective of the SWOT analysis is to help develop a high level action plan. An example of such an analysis is shown in Figure 9.5.

Scenario planning

Although much of the work undertaken during the detailed assessment phase involves reviewing the current situation within the organisations involved in the M&A, the process needs to be future oriented. Before the end of this phase the integration team needs to be able to generate options for the integration strategy as well as measures by which to evaluate them. In many cases the measures will be financial but other, softer, measures may also be used.

Organisations use scenario planning as a tool for strategy development and choice. Building scenarios involves identifying the key factors that influence a business or activity and then making assumptions about change. Since the factors involved are normally inter-connected to a greater or lesser extent, change in one factor will provoke change in another. By changing different key factors to different degrees, alternative pictures of the future, which may occur or could be developed, can be generated. Undertaking such exercises during the detailed assessment phase has a number of advantages. The first is that it requires those involved in developing the integration plan to make explicit the assumptions upon which their proposals are based. The second is that although the M&A itself constitutes a major discontinuity, it should not be allowed to obscure the fact that other significant changes could occur which will impact on the IT function within the business.

For analysing costs and benefits there are multiple techniques. One that is frequently used involves financial scenarios where the various strategic options are compared in terms of investment and cash flow requirements. Depending on the companies involved, a preferred method of calculating the ROI will be used. For a detailed discussion of the various methods (IRR, NPV discounted cash flow or payback period) there are plenty of books available.

In addition the team undertaking the detailed assessment may want to look at the IT integration strategy in a broader context by comparing a number of key indicators such as overall M&A strategy, integration process, IT applications, technology infrastructure, costs, synergies and risks. This technique recognises that not every cost or benefit is easily quantified and the integration strategy and plan may be decided on criteria other than purely financial ones.

A way of using these techniques is to identify a series of possible and desirable scenarios that could be envisaged within the overall M&A strategy and preferred integration models. This defines the demand-side of the IT requirements from a business viewpoint. The second step is to look-at the IT supply side by comparing each scenario with the type of IT applications and IT infrastructure that would be required to support the business requirements. This defines the IT requirements from an IT viewpoint. A third stage involves looking at the costs in each scenario, quantifying the synergies and assessing the risks. Additional indicators can be added to the technique to suit the particular needs of the integration. For example, IT organisation, impact on customers, suppliers and others. A sample of such technique is shown in Figure 9.6.

Risk analysis

A necessary feature of the detailed assessment phase is to analyse the IT risks involved before deciding on a particular integration strategy. For example,

Summary: In moving from current situation to a future position where the Business Vision is realised we have identified 4 main scenarios. Scenario 1 is based on current decentralised country operating model moving towards a divisional model. Scenarios 2, 3 and 4 are based on a single European Operating Model. The main differences are speed and approach. Scenario 2 goal is to develop a standard European System in-house by year 2004. Scenario 3 by 2005 and Scenario 4 by 2003 outsourcing the development.

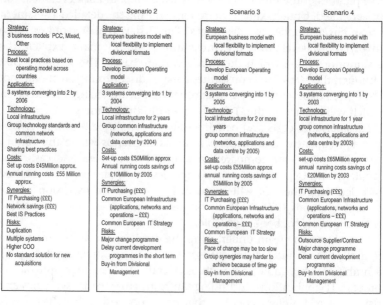

Scenario 1	Scenario 2	Scenario 3	Scenario 4
Strategy: 3 business models PCC, Mixed, Other	Strategy: European business model with local flexibility to implement divisional formats	Strategy: European business model with local flexibility to implement divisional formats	Strategy: European business model with local flexibility to implement divisional formats
Process: Best local practices based on operating model across countries	Process: Develop European Operating model	Process: Develop European Operating model	Process: Develop European Operating model
Application: 3 systems converging into 2 by 2006	Application: 3 systems converging into 1 by 2004	Application: 3 systems converging into 1 by 2005	Application: 3 systems converging into 1 by 2003
Technology: Local infrastructure Group technology standards and common network infrastructure Sharing best practices	Technology: Local infrastructure for 2 years Group common infrastructure (networks, applications and data center by 2004)	Technology: local infrastructure for 2 or more years group common infrastructure (networks, applications and data centre by 2005)	Technology: local infrastructure for 1 year group common infrastructure (networks, applications and data centre by 2003)
Costs: Set up costs £45Million approx. Annual running costs £55 Million approx.	Costs: Set-up costs £50Million approx Annual running costs savings of £10Million by 2005	Costs: set-up costs £55Million approx annual running costs savings of £5Million by 2005	Costs: set-up costs £65Million approx annual running costs savings of £20Million by 2003
Synergies: IT Purchasing (£££) Network savings (£££) Best IS Practices	Synergies: IT Purchasing (£££) Common European Infrastructure (applications, networks and operations – £££) Common European IT Strategy	Synergies: IT Purchasing (£££) Common European Infrastructure (applications, networks and operations – £££) Common European IT Strategy	Synergies: IT Purchasing (£££) Common European Infrastructure (applications, networks and operations – £££) Common European IT Strategy
Risks: Duplication Multiple systems Higher COO No standard solution for new acquisitions	Risks: Major change programme Delay current development programmes in the short term Buy-in from Divisional Management	Risks: Pace of change may be too slow Group synergies may harder to achieve because of time gap Buy-in from Divisional Management	Risks: Outsource Supplier/Contract Major change programme Derail current development programmes Buy-in from Divisional Management

Figure 9.6   Scenario planning example

in a past consulting assignment working for a client in the retail industry the IT risks at the acquired company were seen as a serious threat to the success of the acquisition. This threat was perceived to lie in the obsolescence of the acquired company's systems and their potential threat to support future growth, one of the key reasons for the acquisition in the first place. The identification of such a significant risk narrowed the options open to the CIO and shaped the integration strategy that was adopted.

In this case a useful technique for analysing the main IT risks was developed. From the data collected in step 1 of this phase a list of main IT issues is identified. These issues might relate amongst others to a perceived lack of IT system functionality in key areas such as automatic stock replenishment, an inadequate warehousing system and insufficient price control. Such system issues may have occurred over time due to both external and internal factors. Examples of the former include strong business growth, and the effect of competitors' superior IT systems in the market place which, for example, allow for better stock availability through automatic replenishment. Among the latter are factors such as manual processes, a spreadsheet culture, and informal working practices.

Having identified the main systems issues and their causes the technique then involves analysing the potential risks and their consequences in terms of costs and the effect on the IT organisation. In the example referred to above it turned out that the IT system issues posed a clear threat in financial terms because of potential loss of sales, increased running IT costs and the need for further investment in new IT systems. The threat also impacted the ability of the IT department to provide the required service to stores and distribution operations and in turn this was affecting the morale of the IT department, which was experiencing considerable workload and was suffering from a poor image. Once the above issues and the risks associated with them had been identified and analysed a clear integration strategy was developed to minimise them. A diagrammatic example of the use of the risk analysis technique applied to the example discussed above is shown in Figure 9.7.

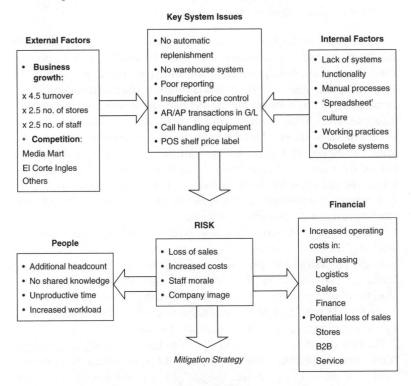

Figure 9.7 Risk analysis model: example

Optimisation assessment

One key driver for the CIO in charge of the acquisition or merger in the first 100 days is to understand what he/she is taking on in terms of IT infrastructure and how to combine it with his/her own in a way that optimises the investment from a financial viewpoint. During the assessment the CIO will seek to obtain answers to questions such as:

• What is the IT spend?
• What is the aggregate IT spending by user?
• What is each company's previous IT investment philosophy?
• Does this philosophy reflect a centralised or distributed computing profile?
• Does this profile reflect computing centricity or network constraints?
• In which aspects of IT do the greatest challenges lie?
• Which initiatives or projects will yield optimum economic impact?
• Where are the quick savings?
• Where are the long-term savings and benefits?

In order to understand the financial structure of synergies to be exploited through the M&A, the CIO needs to identify and classify the various opportunities (projects) from which it would be possible to achieve savings. For example, would combining the two companies' networks produce any savings? Should the two ERP systems be consolidated into one? If so, what savings could be expected over what timeframe? What aspects of the combined operations should be retained and which ones outsourced and what savings can be expected? Is it realistic to reduce the number of IT suppliers, and if so, what are the risks to be taken? Would there be quick savings? A helpful technique to analyse and present the answers to the above questions is by means of constructing an impact assessment diagram.

This technique developed by IBM (Gulati 2002) is a useful way of assessing the two companies' IT infrastructures and their underlying business objectives and processes over a 3 year time-frame (this time frame is considered as the norm for the M&A IT assessment). Optimisation Assessment is also a good technique for examining each company's IT spending profile and helping to identify potential gaps as well as opportunities for the integrated organisation.

The first step in using this technique is to list out the key projects that could generate savings. These savings should be quantified in monetary terms and their likely savings 'pegged' in a time-frame fashion. The technique (explained in detailed below) divides these savings into two axes: high and low (vertical axis) and simple and complex to achieve (horizontal axis). The horizontal axis also denotes time (e.g. simple implementation is assumed to be 6 months or less whereas complex implementation denotes up to 36 months. The projects and their savings are then entered in each of the four quadrants depending on their cost savings and their timing in terms of achievement. This information is then summarised on an impact assessment diagram as shown in Figure 9.8.

Figure 9.8 highlights where savings can be made in the integration process. The top right quadrant represents where there are quick savings over a period of 6 months. These are cost reduction initiatives that help to address the integration of IT infrastructure and consolidate

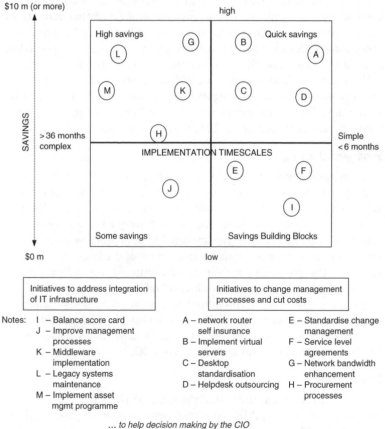

Notes: I – Balance score card
         J – Improve management
              processes
         K – Middleware
              implementation
         L – Legacy systems
              maintenance
         M – Implement asset
              mgmt programme

A – network router
     self insurance
B – Implement virtual
     servers
C – Desktop
     standardisation
D – Helpdesk outsourcing

E – Standardise change
     management
F – Service level
     agreements
G – Network bandwidth
     enhancement
H – Procurement
     processes

... to help decision making by the CIO

Source: Adapted from the Gulah (2002).

Figure 9.8   Impact diagram showing savings

management processes and technology. In the example shown in the diagram initiatives to consolidate and standardise the desktop environment (C) or outsourcing the help desk (D) will represent quick savings.

The top left quadrant represents long-term high savings to be achieved over a period of 36 months. These are initiatives to change management processes (e.g. legacy system maintenance) and to further consolidate/ integrate IT assets and people (e.g. increase network bandwidth). These savings are long term because they are complicated to implement.

The bottom left quadrant represents long-term medium savings. Similarly to quadrant 2 these are initiatives that improve change management processes over the long term (e.g. procurement processes and project management). Like other long-term savings they are complex to achieve. In the case of smaller savings at the bottom of this quadrant, the costs of complex implementation may outweigh potential benefits and the project is financially not viable. It may nonetheless be pursued for other reasons, for example, to improve project management procedures or as part of a cultural change programme in the newly merged company.

The bottom right quadrant represents those short-term initiatives that may involve small initial savings but help to build for the future, known as building blocks. Examples include developing service level agreements (F) and introducing the balanced scorecard (I).

Synergies charting

One key objective for the CIO in the final stages of the detailed assessment is to summarise the IT synergies and formulate a plan of action to achieve them. There are many ways of doing this but one of the most effective is a simple illustrative chart such as the one shown in Figure 9.9.

In this chart the key synergies are listed in rank order by each business area. With each synergy comes an assessment of the likely benefits to be achieved, the potential issues to be encountered, the action required and which area of the business or individual is responsible for achieving them. This chart can be presented to the M&A executive team and represents a clear communication and action plan. The chart can be modified to include other useful things such as target dates, dependencies, to suit the individual requirements of the CIO.

Deliverables

The key deliverables at the end of the detailed assessment phase are the integration strategy and the corresponding integration plan supported by analyses of the current and future situation. The integration strategy should spell out what the new IT operating environment is to be (see Box 9.4), based on the profile of the acquired company.

Business Area	Synergy	Benefits	Issues	Action required	Responsibility	Target date
Purchasing	High	Lower price from supplier. Single supplier interface	3 systems. Multiple links to supply	Define and agree European Purchasing Policy	Purchasing	Mar 02
Merchandising Planning	Medium	Improve group forecasting, planning, route to market	Intake based on regional model. Consolidation complexity	Define and agree European plan	Merchandising	April 02
Inventory management	Medium	Better product availability, stock management, lower working capital	Multiple operating models. Cannot source regionally	Define and agree European plan	Supply Chain	Mar 02
Merchandising	Low	Marginal	Local practice will be preferred. Common product codes	Local decision. Group standard on product codes	Merchandising	Nov 02

Figure 9.9   Synergies chart: example

Box 9.4   Assessment: typical questions addressed (2)

1. What is the current IT strategy?
2. What type of organization do they have, who is accountable for what?
3. What processes do they have?
4. What are the It assets and how well are they used?
5. What are their computing and storage capabilities?
6. What is their network coverage and bandwidth capacity?
7. What applications and data are used, where, and on which platform?
8. What is their systems delivery record and how much does it cost?
9. Who are the main it users?
10. What is the it spending profile?
11. What are the IT strengths, weaknesses, opportunities and threats of the company being assessed?

The integration plan should focus on delivering the integration strategy objectives in the agreed timeframe, within budget and with the allocated resources. Because the emphasis is likely to be on results and speed it is useful to identify the 'quick wins' as early as possible. We saw some examples of these in the impact diagram example. However, it is important to be aware of 'trade-offs' between short-term and long-term objectives. By the fact that short-term objectives dominate the M&A agenda it is easier to concentrate on short-term gains without thinking of the risks of such an approach. An example of this is to be found in the history of C2 (see Box 9.5).

Box 9.5   Short-term thinking: some of the risks

C2's early approach to their first foreign acquisitions was to change little in their acquired subsidiaries giving them a great deal of autonomy. From an IT viewpoint the decision was to: 'let them have their own systems'. The result of this autonomy was a proliferation of incompatible systems which were unique in each country and required specialist IT staff to maintain them at high cost. After years of struggling to get incompatible systems to 'talk to each other' the parent company changed its strategy towards standard systems in each country. This decision came about as a result of management recognizing that the incompatible systems were costing the group dearly in terms of lost income because of lack of flexibility to serve its customers and high It costs which at the time were considered much higher that any other company operating in the same industry.

Source: Extracts from case 2.

Finally, in presenting the integration strategy and plan it is never wise to assume that there is a 'common view' of things. The proposals will appear differently and be interpreted differently by those in different parts of the organisation and by those in the acquiring and acquired or merged company. In international transactions it is not safe to assume a common view is shared by all countries. If a common solution across countries is sought, the integration team may need to be prepared to modify aspects of the implementation to accommodate cultural differences and achieve comparable goals.

The detailed assessment phase is completed when the integration strategy and implementation plan have been accepted and signed off by those responsible for the M&A. Generally the CIO will obtain the sign off for the proposed strategy and plan together with agreed budgets, timings and resources from the team in charge of the overall M&A. On certain occasions the decision may need to be taken above this level at the main board. For example, if the detailed assessment phase has uncovered integration problems with significant cost implications or if integration has called into question the existing IT strategy.

10
Integration

Arguably integration is the most important phase of the whole M&A process. This phase is action-oriented and requires a strong delivery focus. From an IT viewpoint the CIO needs to perform a balancing act between managing the transition to the new operating environment and keeping current systems going until such time as the new infrastructure, systems and organisation can take over. This balance, between development and operational activity, creates a number of challenges for the CIO that have been discussed at length in Chapters 4, 5 and 6.

In Chapter 9 we noted that at the end of the detailed assessment the CIO will have presented the main IT strategic choices for achieving integration. These should have been agreed with the Board, or with the executive management group responsible for the full M&A project. In this chapter we take the integration strategy as the starting point and discuss the following:

- key aspects of drawing the integration plan in detail
- key aspects of the integration activities in the plan
- the monitoring and control of the integration process
- helpful tools and techniques to support the CIO during this phase

Planning

From a high-level planning viewpoint, the key activities in the integration phase are to do with implementing major strategic change (unless the strategic option is no integration). The bulk of the activities focus on making changes to the following:

1. Existing IT infrastructure (hardware, software, networks and communication systems).

2. Associated physical assets (servers, desktops, laptops, printers, application software, databases, email, web sites, local area networks, wide area networks, routers, telephone systems and others).
3. Human resources (IT staff, roles and responsibilities and working locations).
4. IT supplier arrangements (contracts, service provision, price and supplier status).
5. Internal business users and external customers (business processes, application systems and operating procedures).

A high level view of these activities is shown in Figure 10.1.

As we heard repeatedly from the CIOs in our research, a key lesson learned is to make sure that the high level plan is translated into a more detailed plan covering individual activities and tasks. A typical IT integration plan for a medium to large M&A project would contain several hundred activities. The more detailed the plan is the less the risk of forgetting something major. As with most plans the closer the horizon, the more important is the detail. An example of the first page of the first 4 weeks' IT integration plan is shown in Figure 10.2

Before the detailed plan is drawn the CIO would be wise to secure good understanding and support from the organisation for his or her implementation plans. In such a strategic project it is essential to write

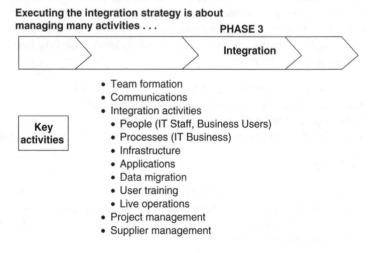

. . . to achieve integration and deliver the expected M&A synergies

Figure 10.1 Integration phase: activity overview

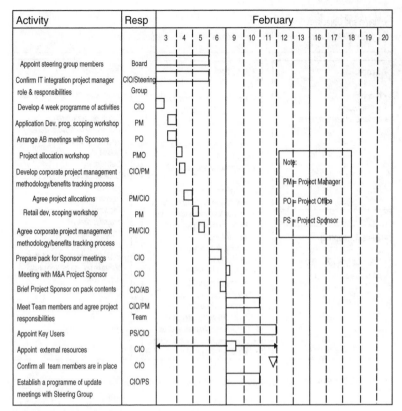

IT Integration Work Stream – First 4 Weeks Programme of Activities (Sheet 1 of 4)

Figure 10.2   IT integration detail plan: example

down the key project elements before the project kicks off. A helpful technique for doing this is the project charter, see Figure 10.3.

The project charter is a formal document that explains the following:

- what needs to be achieved (key objectives)
- what is covered and what is not (scope)
- who is responsible for what (roles, responsibilities and accountabilities)
- when the project needs to achieve key milestones (phases, activities and target dates)
- the challenges ahead (risks, issues and contingencies)
- the benefits to be achieved (synergies)
- criteria to suit the specifics of each company's situation.

- **Vision and Objectives:**
  - Integrated MIS function and infrastructure from both companies which provides a platform for growth.

- **Scope**	- **Activities**	- **Key issues**
• IS function • IS infrastructure • Implication of M&A programme	• Assemble integration team including consultants and contractors • Communicate integration plan to all MIS staff • Complete and announce new MIS organisation • Confirm overall integration MIS budget • Confirm technical infrastructure • Confirm systems integration strategy and short term manual workarounds • Decide on business processes changes if any • Complete data integration plan • Establish KPI's • Integrate customer databases • Integrate product databases • Reporting consolidation plan • Migration to single data centre • Review disaster recovery plans • Complete MIS governance review • Confirm supplier contracts including outsourcing opportunities	• Identification and retention of key staff • Maintaining service during migration • Penalty clauses in contracts • Compatibility of hardware, operating systems and applications • Multiple sites • Staff relocation • Understanding and managing current initiatives • Scarcity of key skills • Interdependency of business and MIS integration needs • Managing tension between extent and cost of integration • Retraining technical staff and users • Managing risk and satisfying audit requirements

- **Benefits (approx)**		
• Headcount (year 2/3)	£6.0m	
• Licences, etc.	£1.5m	

Figure 10.3   Systems integration project charter: example

The project charter is a guiding document and should be consulted throughout the project.

The role of the CIO during the integration planning activity is essential. Depending on the size of the M&A and the CIO's previous experience he or she might be expected to act as the project manager, programme manager or integration director. Whatever the role chosen his or her planning, organising and leading skills will be required to the full.

Executing the plan

In the course of implementing the integration plan the CIO will need to execute IT and business related activities. In the former the main ones are:

- IT Infrastructure
- application systems

- IT organisation
- security

In the latter the main ones are:

- business processes
- business users (internal)
- external customers
- IT suppliers

The type of infrastructure changes required vary from company to company but in most M&A transactions the CIO will be dealing with hardware rationalisation and optimisation as discussed in the previous chapter. Generally the CIO will be implementing changes such as:

- rationalisation of hardware platforms (e.g. desktop, servers)
- simplification or elimination of differences in hardware technology (e.g. different versions of operating systems)
- consolidation or creation of new operating facilities (e.g. data centres)
- expansion of network bandwidth requirements (e.g. wide area network)
- linkage telephone systems and web sites (e.g. joint telephone directories)
- adoption of a single email system (e.g. Microsoft Outlook)

In dealing with these changes the CIO will come across, and will need to deal successfully with, different technology platforms, shortages of technical skills and different suppliers to mention just a few areas. Even if the CIO is technically competent he or she needs to be supported by a strong technical team with high levels of problem solving capability to resolve all the technical issues.

In the software area the major changes normally occur in the area of application system interfaces and often in the replacement of old legacy systems. The CIO will be dealing with the non-trivial task of developing new system links or implementing new applications in a very short period of time. The issues of rationalisation of applications systems are normally harder and take more time to resolve than those involving hardware. As discussed in Chapter 5 a range of other issues may creep in as a result of incompatible technology, different development tools, and obsolete legacy systems. In dealing with these changes the CIO will need to select carefully his or her application team and make sure that communications among the two technical IT departments are open to allow technical knowledge to be exchanged freely.

In most successful M&As the changes related to people take place early in the integration process. From an IT view point it is helpful if the CIO has already announced his or her new team before the IT integration starts. This is particularly important because during the integration project everyone needs to concentrate on the integration tasks rather than being worried about their future. If the CIO has not already dealt with this issue it must be seen as a high priority. Typical issues related to people changes during this phase are retention, skills shortages, contract negotiation, technical sabotage and differences in country labour law and practices. To deal with the personal, contractual and legal issues the CIO should work closely with the HR Department and with the rest of the M&A team.

Security is an area that is seldom mentioned during an M&A integration project. From an IT perspective security has several dimensions:

1. Physical security in terms of access to data centres and computing facilities.
2. Computer or network access.
3. Access to a particular application or service.
4. Technical security within the IT organisation itself.

From the CIO's perspective all four need to be checked and dealt with in order to minimise the risks to computer information and facilities of the two companies. It is not unheard of that a disgruntled IT employee commits fraud or sabotage after leaving the company following an M&A because the company had been lax in tightening security after his or her departure. Security is also important from the point of view of external audit; CFOs and Chairmen get nervous when the auditors mention in their report that IT security is not adequate. In the case of a foreign M&A, particularly in countries where security is known to be lax, the risks are much higher. The CIO should take no chances in this area.

In addition to IT changes the CIO will be dealing with other changes that are outside the technical spectrum. Business process change is often required as part of the integration project. This activity is normally driven by the business and requires the CIO to respond. Like IT changes, business process changes have a potentially high impact. If confronted with this situation the CIO needs to work closely with the business functional areas affected by the process change and dovetail these changes with the IT systems. Ideally business changes should be made before the new IT systems are implemented. Hence the CIO should press for quick decisions from the business on business process changes at the beginning of the integration process.

With the introduction of IT changes during the integration project may come changes in business users' working practices. It is important that the CIO makes allowances in his or her integration plan for user training to adopt the new IT systems. This provides a good opportunity for both organisations to work together and get to know each other and for IT to build new relations with the acquired business users.

During the transition between old and new the CIO needs to manage the business users' expectations. For example, in the acquired company some business users will be unhappy with the service provided by their previous IT department and will expect an instant improvement with the new IT organisation. By contrast, those users in the acquired company that were happy with the IT services before will be worried that the new IT organisation may change their favourite systems. Similarly, in the acquiring company some business users may face anxiety and uncertainty, fearing that the new IT organisation will be preoccupied with solving the IT problems of the acquired company rather than meeting their own needs.

Meeting external customer expectations during the transition is also an important objective for the CIO. External customers are often suspicious of mergers and may use the changes as an excuse to buy elsewhere. The last thing a CIO wants to do, as discussed in Chapter 6, is to provide them with a reason for them to stop being customers.

Changing IT suppliers is often a consequence of new company ownership. Savings in the area of IT purchasing often account for 5–10 per cent of the total IT synergies. However, while this is an area targeted for change CIOs are often reluctant to move quickly in this area. The CIO's primary concern is to ensure an orderly changeover from one supplier to another. The commercial advantages, although important, will normally be a second consideration. The decision to retain or change existing IT suppliers is normally made during the assessment phase after careful evaluation of current support service, quality and price. During the changeover process the CIO needs to maintain good relationships with existing suppliers and ensure that those whose contracts are terminated are treated fairly so that operational risks are minimised.

Monitoring and control

Monitoring and control activities are an integral part of project management. These activities are aimed at:

- Achieving the project objectives.
- Hitting the agreed milestones on time.
- Achieving the objectives within the allocated budget.
- Maintaining continuity of business operation.
- Tracking progress against the plan and reviewing the milestones as the project gets rolled out.
- Taking corrective action to resolve any contingencies.
- Reporting to the M&A Executive Team and to the Board as necessary.

In order to monitor and control the integration project most companies adopt a project management control framework. This framework is important to control the key integration activities and reduce the implementation risks. The project management control framework is normally built around individual project charters such as the one shown in Figure 10.3. This is a top-down planning approach essential for large M&A projects. Within this framework a formal reporting and accountability system operates with each layer responsible for ensuring that the layer beneath meets their targets and delivers their part of the integration plan.

The advantages of such frameworks is that all the key integration activities are monitored against the agreed objectives as laid out in the project charters, including the business synergies that each project is to deliver. Key decisions are then made and communicated by the Steering Committee. The whole approach is orderly managed and is essential for large M&A integration projects. Smaller M&A projects may not require this approach to the same extent but the framework is equally valid for small M&A integration projects. An overview of such a framework is shown in Figure 10.4.

Within this framework the CIO is in a position to monitor regularly the IT integration activities against the agreed timescales, budgets and quality parameters that have been agreed. Through this mechanism the CIO is also able to coordinate efforts and resources for other integration initiatives in other functional areas. In a large integration the involvement of IT may expand to several business or geographical areas and the framework also serves as a good tracking and coordinating tool.

In order to monitor and control the integration project companies also adopt a project steering organisation similar to the one shown in

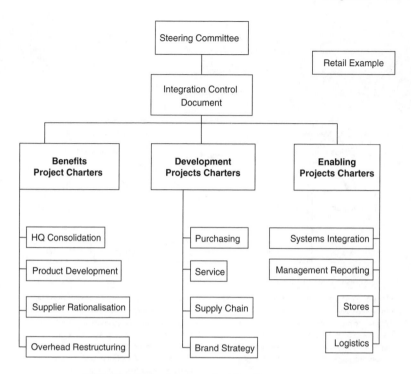

... With project charters to manage the integration programme

Figure 10.4   Integration project management framework: example

Figure 10.5 in tandem with the project control framework. In this type of organisation the Steering Committee makes policy and strategic decisions regarding the entire M&A project. As an important member of the Steering Committee, the CIO has the forum to report back on the IT integration project and highlight any critical implementation issues affecting IT. In some cases the CIO will be acting as a project manager for the IT functional area in which his or her reporting will be fairly detailed. In other cases his role may be that of a project sponsor responsible for IT or some other business area in which case he or she will take more of an advisory or executive decision role.

The fundamental objective of the monitoring and control process is to reach a successful integration project. As already mentioned in the previous chapters M&A projects suffer from a number of uncertainties that give rise to contingencies and risk. From an IT view point the CIO will be facing a number of these uncertainties that he or she needs to be

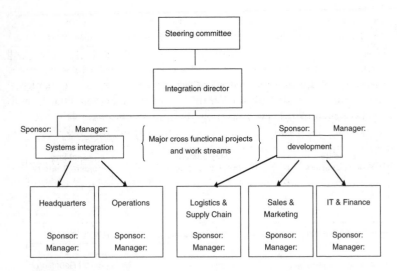

Figure 10.5   M&A integration steering group organisation

prepared for. The main contingencies typically fall into the following categories:

- Time overruns
- Budget overruns
- Resource shortfalls
- Organisational problems
- Changing objectives
- Technical difficulties

We are all aware of the bad publicity that IT projects get in the press when they are late or dramatically over-budget. As a result of the centrality of IT mentioned in previous chapters IT bad news spreads at a surprising speed, even if unfair and out of context. In the M&A context IT has a difficult job and the CIO is working against the clock to achieve the integration activities on time. Time overruns in a typical IT project occur for many different reasons: poor initial time estimates, insufficient clarity of the task in hand, lack of quality resources and many others.

In a M&A IT project time overruns are common because a fair amount of the IT activity in this phase is based on an emerging situation. For example, when dealing with building application system interfaces the amount of technical knowledge about the legacy systems may be incomplete and the IT technical staff designing this part of the project may encounter difficult technical problems that take much longer to resolve than originally planned. A similar situation may happen when dealing with data migration where the Database Administrator (DBA) may encounter problems with system performance that require a long period of 'tuning' before the application can be operational. There are similar potential problems in other IT areas such as network deployment, hardware acquisition and system testing.

As a seasoned manager the CIO would be wise to allow for contingency in his or her time estimates. Regular internal reviews with the IT integration team will reveal any potential time overruns and the CIO will be able to take corrective action before these are exposed at the Steering Committee level. Being prepared does not solve the problem entirely but makes it easier and quicker to deal with when it is encountered.

Budget overruns in an M&A IT project happen though perhaps less frequently than the previous comments about bad news suggest. From a CIO's perspective this is an area that he or she should be clearly focused on. Most budget overruns occur when financial control is neglected. For example, if the initial estimates on integration IT costs are poor, or the expectation is that IT will be done 'on the cheap', then clearly some of the expectations about costs will be unrealistic and the IT initial budget cost will be exceeded. On the other hand, genuine additional IT costs may be encountered as a result of poor planning by the CIO him/herself, time overruns, expensive external IT resources, poor utilisation of internal resources, higher prices for equipment or services and other unforeseen factors.

In this situation the CIO needs to review his or her budget and see where economies and savings can be made to reduce the gap. Sometimes if there are good reasons for the budget overrun the Steering Committee may be able to release further funds to IT. In other cases the CIO may have to reduce the scope of his/her activities in order to remain within budget. This leads to short-term thinking that is very prevalent in an

M&A project as explained in previous chapters. However, cutting corners on expenditure is not always the best strategy as it creates problems further on in time as illustrated in the following example (see Box 10.1).

In the financial area the CIO will be expected to deliver the IT synergies, in particular the 'quick wins'. These include headcount reduction, savings on IT purchasing, rationalisation of hardware equipment and economies of scale efficiencies in the way the IT department of the combined organisations operates. Some of the savings during an M&A will be short term such as headcount reduction. Others will only be achieved on a long-term basis as explained in Chapter 9. From a CIO's perspective it is important to note that some of these savings may be difficult to achieve because they are dependent on the business 'playing ball'. Such savings may take longer to achieve in a changing environment where staff and management turnover are common. For example, implementing desktop standards may take longer than expected and not achieve the same savings as originally planned because some users may take longer than anticipated to become proficient. As a result some headcount savings may not be achieved. In this situation the CIO should say upfront that the achievement of these benefits is a shared responsibility with the business. The accountability factor in these grey areas is not always clear but the CIO should stand his or her ground here.

Resource contingency is an area the CIO must plan for. The problems related to IT staff leaving after an M&A have been discussed at length already in Chapter 6. From a contingency view these problems are

---

Box 10.1   Budget constraints cause loss of business

In one of the consultancy assignments undertaken by one of the authors some years ago it was discovered that the IT service provided at one of the small subsidiaries of a multinational was poor and the business users were unhappy. Under closer inspection it was discovered that the problem originated since the parent company had acquired this particular subsidiary a year previously. The problem was that due to the poor performance of the email server, everyone was suffering heavy delays and the sales people were complaining that they were losing business. This was a company in the recruitment industry where most of the business is done by email and requires a fast turnaround. When the consultant asked the IT Manager why he had not replaced the server with a more powerful one, the answer came: 'this was noticed at the due diligence stage and we were told that it would be replaced once the company was acquired, but when the acquisition was completed I was told that there was no enough money in the budget and the sever needed to carry on for a bit longer'.

difficult to plan for as they are dependent on individual circumstances. The CIO along with all the other M&A managers will not have the luxury of having a surplus of resources, therefore the mitigation is around knowledge sharing and team working. If a key IT person leaves the integration team and he or she had unique technical knowledge, then a replacement is unlikely to be found quickly or easily. This is a case of 'prevention is better than cure' and the CIO in the assessment phase should take care that he or she is not exposed unduly by tightening the contractual arrangements made with key staff. Other typical resource contingencies during the integration phase are lack of adequate IT resources and/or skills and poor quality. If the CIO faces this situation at the integration stage it is likely to be as a result of poor or non-existing due diligence or assessment. Recovery is to deal with the situation in the most expedient way by changing or acquiring more resources. If this is not an option the CIO should at least flag it as an issue at the Steering Committee level.

By far the greatest challenge facing the CIO from a contingency viewpoint is likely to be the organisation itself. In implementing strategic change the CIO will come across resistance to change, changing organisational objectives, political infighting ('them and us' syndrome), unreliable information on which to base immediate actions, complexity and many others. For example, the need to reduce complexity by phasing implementation is something that the CIO frequently encounters in an M&A integration project. The roll-out of standard desktop systems has already been mentioned as a quick win. However, if multiple locations are involved, deciding in which order the implementation is to proceed requires a good understanding of the business users and local IT. In an M&A transaction this is rarely possible because the two organisations have just met. Putting one location before another may create not only technical issues but political and organisational issues as well. The complexity is then compounded if the M&A transaction involves international locations, different cultures, different customs and languages.

In the fulfilment of the integration project the CIO often needs to make decision on the hoof with less than adequate information. In the example quoted, sharing the IT resources between both organisations and making each IT department responsible for implementing their own patch may be an acceptable compromise. However, at the end of the day it is the CIO of the parent company who bears the risk that project may be delayed, costs escalate or the technology does not work and the organisation suffers operational disruption as a result. Contingency planning is strong card in the CIO's hand which he or she must be ready to play whenever necessary.

A different type of contingency typical of an M&A integration project relates to changing of the organisation's objectives. The chances of this happening increases with the length and complexity of the integration project. From an IT view point a not uncommon problem is when the scope or complexity of the IT activities are changed during the course of the integration project as the following example illustrates.

> One of our challenges was that the scope of the project grew. Initially we underestimated its complexity. The system we were converting to was a one company system but we were dealing with 2 companies in five different countries, with different regulatory policies and geography. It meant that IT needed to be flexible and responsive to changing requirements. If we had not got a detailed integration plan to start with we could not have succeeded in the short time available. (McDonald 2003)

Changing the goal posts is sometimes inevitable but the CIO should work closely with the M&A sponsor to minimise this area of risk. In any case he or she should make it clear to the members of the Steering Committee the implications of such changes of course for the implementation's resources, time and costs.

Last but not least there are technical contingencies. In the area of IT these are inevitable and should be planned for as much as is possible. Reducing technical novelty, implementing standard systems that have been implemented before, sharing technical knowledge among IT staff and good IT governance in the IT change process are all measures that reduce technical risks. As already mentioned the best protection from a CIO perspective is to go into the integration project with a strong and competent IT technical team and an established IT technology strategy and policies. The more technically competent the CIO is the more likely that these risks will be identified early enough in the integration process and be avoided. Technical contingencies can be serious and cause severe operational discontinuity, which is why sometimes IT projects hit the headlines. The wise CIO will have a technical contingency plan ready just in case; ignoring the issue is done at the CIO's peril. No CIO worth his/ her salt enjoys standing in front of the Steering Committee to relate that he or she has encountered a technical contingency that was not prepared for.

Concluding remarks

The involvement of the CIO throughout the integration process is critical irrespective of the particular role played. He or she is a catalyst for change and the organisation as a whole will be relying on his or her leadership, managerial capability, technical competence and communication skills to deliver a successful IT integration. One particular customer that the CIO needs to satisfy is the CEO, whose reputation will also depend on the successful implementation of the M&A project. In career terms the CIO has a wonderful opportunity to impress his or her boss by delivering a successful project. Some of the CIOs who have reached the enviable position of being invited to the M&A table before the M&A acquisition process starts, are in this position because they have earned their reputation in previous integration projects.

At the end of the integration process a formal review process should take place, which is the subject of the next chapter. To finish this chapter we return to the subject of action orientation with which we started. The entire detailed plan comes to nothing if it cannot be delivered. However, while the plan may be the road map, the CIO is the driver.

11
Post-integration Review

Good project management involves undertaking regular reviews throughout a project as well as a final review, which looks back across the project as a whole and measures the benefits achieved against the objectives set. The final review may be combined with or may precede a review of the lessons learned, which can lead to improvements in practice in the future. However the review is organised, the important point is that it is taken seriously and given importance. Unfortunately this is not always the case and as a result some companies pay a heavy price in the longer term when they are next involved in an M&A.

Integration following an M&A is usually a multifaceted process encompassing a set of projects and sub-projects. Some of these projects will have longer time-scales than others. The question therefore arises of when integration can be said to be complete. For each of the individual projects this may be established relatively easily, but for the integration process as a whole the point may be rather more arbitrary. Nevertheless, at some point, often 6–12 months after the main integration projects have been completed, a review of what has been learned should be initiated.

The post-integration review needs to capture the M&A experience that otherwise would be lost at a point when people still have the experience fresh in their minds but at the same time are able to reflect upon the experience with some degree of objectivity. Timing is important as a review carried out too soon may lack perspective and look only at the most short-term features of integration; on the other hand a review delayed for too long may be hard to carry out once the key teams involved in the M&A have been disbanded and may be overshadowed by other events. An overview of the main activities involved is shown in Figure 11.1.

A Post-Integration Review is a formal process...

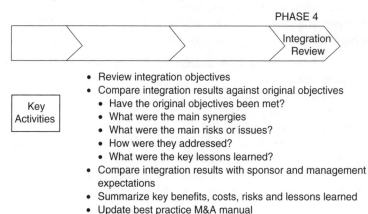

PHASE 4

Integration Review

Key Activities

- Review integration objectives
- Compare integration results against original objectives
  - Have the original objectives been met?
  - What were the main synergies
  - What were the main risks or issues?
  - How were they addressed?
  - What were the key lessons learned?
- Compare integration results with sponsor and management expectations
- Summarize key benefits, costs, risks and lessons learned
- Update best practice M&A manual

... to allow the M&A benefits and lessons learned to be quantified

Figure 11.1 Post-integration review phase: activity overview

The post-integration review is a reflective type of activity that looks back at the merger once the dust has settled and business has returned to normal. It should never be a witch hunt, but rather a pragmatic look at the events of the merger from beginning to end with the view to learning and quantifying the main benefits and documenting the findings. It is important that the post-integration review takes an objective view of the M&A experience and therefore should ideally be done, or at least facilitated, by someone independent. An independent view can be obtained from outside the organisation from an external consultant or may be obtained from inside the organisation from internal audit or other functional area sponsored by a senior manager. If the M&A were large and complex, a review team of appropriate size will be needed to undertake the task effectively.

An important distinction should be drawn by the review team between measuring the achievement of objectives and synergies and reviewing the processes adopted to achieve them. Clearly the two are linked but the first enquiry answers the question, did we achieve what we set out to do? And the second answers the question; did we do it in the most effective way? The first set of questions is often linked to another type of post-implementation review which asks the question, what else needs to be done in order to benefit from the project that has been undertaken? This is an essential part of the movement from implementation to post-implementation as the merged organisation seeks to develop and improve further.

In answering the first set of questions the review team should focus on issues such as:

- Did the M&A IT integration strategy work? If so, how did IT meet the original objectives?
- Were there any IT synergies? Which ones? How were they achieved?
- What were the main benefits? (soft and hard)
- What were the risks taken? Did they pay off?
- What were the key IT and business issues? How were they addressed?
- What were the IT integration benefits? How were they achieved? What was the total financial value of these benefits?
- What were the IT integration costs? How were they achieved? What was the total cost?
- Were management expectations met? How?

This exercise quantifies the benefits of M&A and learns from the experience by recording the best management practices that are invaluable for next time when another M&A is contemplated. For example, in C3 the post implementation review identified three key improvement areas before undertaking the next acquisition: early and detailed IT due diligence, early IT involvement in the M&A process and good project management.

The post-implementation review team should look at benefits in the context of the original M&A objectives. Although this activity occurs at the end of the M&A process, it is dependent on how well the original business vision and benefits were defined and communicated in earlier phases of the merger. One of the reasons why the post-implementation phase is often not completed effectively is because the original benefits context was never defined or the definition was not done well. An example of this problem is illustrated in C1. Lack of IT due diligence and an integration process that failed to clearly quantify the IT synergies left the acquiring company with no clear measurement for assessing the results of the merger. The fact that the IT integration project ran into multiple issues indicated a lack of understanding about how to integrate the two companies.

(Note: although the above example reflected the M&A thinking and current practices of the late 1970's it should not be discarded as irrelevant in today's practices as it is clearly the case that companies continue to make very similar mistakes)

The focus of the second set of questions should be rather different. Their purpose is not to measure performance against target, but rather to take a learning organisation approach to the experience of M&A. Writers

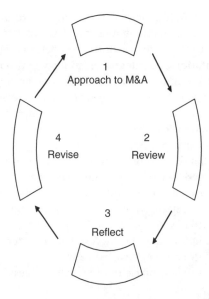

Source: Based on Kolb (1984).
Figure 11.2 Learning from experience

on successful M&A's stress the important role that experience of previous M&A's plays in ensuring smooth integration and the realisation of benefits. 'Experience ... seems to bear fruit when the acquirer is able to discern what knowledge will be useful and appropriate in the case of a new acquisition' (Very 2004). To be valuable, experience must be considered reflectively and must influence subsequent policies and behavior. Learning is often portrayed as a cycle (Kolb 1984) such as that drawn in Figure 11.2.

The key questions that this part of the review will focus on are:

- What went well that should be repeated next time?
- What could have been done better or differently?
- What are the key lessons learned for the next M&A?

To ascertain the answers to both sets of questions a number of approaches are typically used such as:

- review of original plans and targets
- analysis of interim reports produced
- user questionnaires (internal and external)
- workshops
- one to one interviews
- observation and reflection on experience

Experience shows that people may be reluctant to talk about merger problems or difficulties that may reflect negatively on them unless they have left the company or are one of the competitors. Those responsible for the implementation and integration strategy may tend to exaggerate the benefits. Caution must be exercised when reviewing the benefits as seen by the management involved as it is often the case that they tend to be optimistically biased. As multiple post implementation review surveys demonstrate using executive opinions only as a benchmark for success needs to be questioned (Pautler 2003).

On the other hand, among users and those whose work has been disrupted or changed by the M&A, there may be an over-critical evaluation of what has been achieved and how it was done. To counter this, a clear data-gathering strategy, which draws evidence from different sources and triangulates, is important. In practice also a combination of the above techniques may be necessary in order to capture the complexity of information and varied views.

This post merger review phase has two deliverables:

- a management report or reports with key findings and lessons learned
- best practices for future M&A IT work

The management report, or reports, should outline the key findings to the questions posed above and make recommendations for future actions. These reports, provided they are used and acted upon, are invaluable documents for future M&As and help to build a repertoire of best practices within the company. Where M&As are viewed as a sporadic or ad hoc activity it is much more difficult to incorporate the lessons learned into company practice.

Although it may appear that many companies are not very good at formally reviewing the merger and experience transaction there is plenty of evidence to suggest that this is an important area for companies to review as the benefits from such an exercise are considerable. Companies such as Intel, General Electric, Cisco and Hewlett Packard have well oiled M&A integration teams where IT is an integral part of them. These companies could be argued to be in the acquisition and disposal market making a large number of M&As transactions on an annual basis and therefore it makes sense that they have a dedicated M&A team. However, it can be argued that even in the case of smaller or less frequent transactions it is justified to review the experience and learn from it.

Intel's example also shows that the work done by the M&A team can yield other benefits often not obvious. For example, as a result of multiple reviews in their M&A work Intel found that the M&A activity was transferable to divestitures, so when their acquisition activity petered out they were able to adapt their M&A processes and procedures to divestitures avoiding their initial 'cross functional struggles that accompanied their original efforts' (Intel 2002).

Many companies, including large international organisations, have learned the hard way about this topic by repeating previous mistakes. However those who have carried out a post implementation review have in some cases enjoyed unanticipated benefits from the activity. Such benefits are illustrated by the following examples. A successful M&A can be a source of competitive advantage not only because of the new size and combined strength in the market place but also because it can be seen as an indication of the quality of management involved (see Boxes 11.1, 11.2 and 11.3).

The review process presents the CIO with the opportunity to record the key points of the M&A IT project and summarises them in a way that they can be re-used and updated with newer experiences as they are gained. In the same way as this book presents material from the cases, the process of review means that the CIO can begin to develop their own

---

Box 11.1 Success story: technology merger

In 2003 one of the managers involved in the recent merger between Hewlett Packard and Compaq gave a presentation at a professional seminar describing the issues raised by the merger and the process followed by HP. The presentation not only informed the audience about the integration but also advertised the companies' success and approach which turn reflected positively on the quality of their strategy and management.

Source: HP Presentation, Oct. 2004.

Box 11.2 Success story: bank merger

Another example of successfully selling the success of their M&A experience is that of the merger of Royal Bank of Scotland and National Westminster Bank in UK. One of RBS IT managers claimed that £350 m IT annual savings had been possible by a clear and detailed integration plan, a 'can do culture' and a technology integration directorate that completed the 3 year integration 6 months ahead of schedule. Professional IT management was portrayed as a clear winner out of this merger.

Source: Watson (2003).

Box 11.3   Success story – oil merger

Following the merger with its previous Italian joint venture partner C16 carried out a post implementation review. From the review findings a set of improvement proposals and best practices were identified. These included: a clear IT strategy before the next merger, a detailed cultural assessment of the target company and clear communications throughout the entire integration process. All these recommendations were implemented in their second merger in Germany and as a result the second merger was much more successful than the first one.

Source: CIO's interview.

'recipe book' of best practices that can be consulted and expanded from personal experience that can be used as best practices.

Many of the key lessons to emerge from post-merger review are unique to the companies involved. However, the cases discussed in this book and the views expressed by CIOs suggest that there are some common themes and lessons relating to process which are reflected in the outcomes of post-integration reviews:

1. *State clearly the expected benefits of the M&A.* Reviews should show a link between strategy and its implementation and the achievement of benefits in an M&A. Where the objectives of M&A have not been specified at the beginning of the process it is guesswork at the review stage to check or quantify the benefits achieved against what it was expected. Unless the achievements can be measured and quantified, the effectiveness of the processes used cannot be demonstrated or evaluated.

2. *IT synergies are important, so document them.* It is often not possible to evaluate the contribution of IT to an M&A effectively because detailed assumptions about IT synergies have not been documented. Furthermore, the invisibility of IT in some transactions results in less being achieved than the potential that exists in the companies involved in the transaction. By articulating more clearly what the IT synergies are, and how they are going to be realised, IT can make a significant contribution in the value of the M&A deal at bidding time and afterwards.

3. *IT risks are important, so document them.* IT is often shown to have been considered as an after thought in an M&A. However, the risks can be substantial in terms of productive hours lost, business lost, and additional expenditure. IT is not normally the deal-maker but can be the deal-breaker if it is not involved effectively in the process.

4. *M&A experience counts.* There is a clear link between previous M&A experience and successful IT integration. If you do not have previous M&A experience the right skills need to be brought in before the integration project is underway. Lack of experience underscores the importance of review and learning from completed projects.

5. *Apply the 80/20 Rule.* The learning from companies that have gone though an M&A IT project many times before is that striking the right balance between perfection and speed is key. Applying the 80/20 rule where 80 per cent is good enough is about right. Attempting to achieve 100 per cent can result in delays that lose the project both focus and commitment. In an M&A context delays can also allow pre-merger issues and power groups to re-establish themselves and further jeopardise the process.

6. *Economies of scale = standardisation.* IT synergies without common standards are much more difficult to achieve. Economies of scale are only possible when same standards are applied. The CIO should not be distracted by the political exigencies of a 'softly softly' approach and multiple standards.

7. *Culture diversity = flexible standards.* IT synergies are more difficult and take longer to achieve (sometimes never can be achieved) in a culturally diverse or cross-border environment. However, while flexible IT standards may be required to cope in such an environment, the CIO must be aware that flexibility and standards are not good bed-fellows.

8. *Friendly versus hostile.* Synergies are more difficult to achieve in a hostile M&A post-integration environment. A hostile environment is not necessarily confined to a technically hostile acquisition. Review demonstrates that dominance of processes by personal agendas, cultural differences and technical disputes all make the IT integration work difficult and less likely to achieve synergies and benefits.

Successful M&A IT integration involves a great deal of planning and the careful execution of a well thought out implementation strategy. People and change management are also important ingredients for being successful. As with any major business change top level executive leadership and commitment will be mandatory. In integrating IT a number of business issues will be uncovered and this requires the understanding and support of the senior management team from both companies.

The process of implementing the M&A IT integration strategy is the culmination of many activities previously planned and executed with clockwork accuracy. This requires a professional approach to strategic change, project management and in some cases experience of international exposure to foreign cultural and languages. Mergers involve the integration of two organisations with their own cultures, which is inevitably a challenging process: the process is doubly challenging when the organisations are operating in different national and global cultures. For example the CIO may face the question of choosing the 'right' language in which to conduct business which exposes the limitations of using only English as the working language in international mergers.

Companies are increasingly relying on the IT synergies following an international M&A to justify the investment to their shareholders. Achieving these synergies is important and can be obtained by a well thought out strategy and rigorous implementation. However, the CIO should always be realistic about calculating the pay back benefits as there are many factors affecting them. For example, IT outsourcing has recently become a common trend post integration to achieve quick pay-back benefits after a merger. Experience shows that these quick savings have long-term contractual clauses linked to them and when these are considered the long-term benefits may be less than anticipated.

Ultimately, the main benefit of IT integration is to take advantage of the combined IT resources from both companies and realise the well known phrase that: 'the value of the whole is greater than the individual parts'. If this is not the case, why bother?

Part IV
Closing

12
The Role of the External Consultant

A consultant is someone that provides expert and professional advice. Many of the characteristics and skills that we discuss here apply generally to any management consultant. The focus here, however, is on the consultant that gives expert and professional advice in the area of IT in the context of an M&A project. The advice may be technical or managerial. Based on our research the use of IT consultants in an M&A project is still limited. Despite the evidence of associated IT risks in an M&A project most companies prefer to go alone rather than use external IT consultants. The main reason seems to be that companies associate consultants with high fees and they believe that using own resources is more cost effective than using consultants.

However, there is a realisation by some companies that IT consultants are important and add value in an M&A project. In the cases where IT consultants have been used their role has been primarily in the technical area during the post integration stage. In a minority of cases where IT consultants have been used in a more strategic role their involvement has been at the pre-acquisition stage and has involved work on IT due diligence, assessment of synergies, strategic options and IT strategy.

Choosing the right IT consultant is not easy and companies can fall into a number of pitfalls when trying to do so. The choice of the right consultant is critical and companies planning an M&A IT project are well advised to plan for this activity early in the M&A process. Best of breed consultancy companies are traditionally the ones that attract the best IT consultants and consequently are the most expensive. First time M&A clients traditionally go for the 'big names' as a sign of quality and security. The more experienced client that has gone through the M&A loop more than once often looks for smaller consultancy firms to resource their IT M&A work and reduce the costs.

The advantages of using consultants

Consultants are hired for a variety or reasons which include: shortage of expertise, shortage of staff, shortage of time, need for an objective point of view or to ensure credibility (McKay 2002).

A summary of commonly cited advantages of consultants is shown in Box 12.1.

The key advantage of using an IT consultant in an M&A project is that he or she brings expertise (technical or management) that is lacking in the client organisation.

Typically this may be in areas such as project management, ERP implementation, database administration, software development and testing, and IT infrastructure. In addition to the technical skills M&A IT consultants can offer a great deal of experience in the planning and implementation of an M&A project. Their expertise in due diligence, synergy assessment, gap analysis, strategic options, IT strategy, programme management, change management and communications are particularly important.

A second area of advantage, perhaps as important as the first one, is to achieve results within the tight deadlines of an M&A project. In a demanding IT environment where internal resources are fully stretched, any major change project is bound to require additional resources for which consultants may be the right approach. 'The reduction of IT staff in the traditional IT department especially in the larger more established shops is also freeing the supply of ready consultants' (Schiesser 2001). Therefore using consultants for M&A projects also takes advantage of favourable conditions on the supply side.

Box 12.1   Advantages of using an IT consultant

1. Reduce risk (get the job done professionally and on time)
2. M&A IT project experience
3. Readily available expertise (technical and management)
4. Readily available quality resource and skills
5. Cost effective way of dealing with one-off projects
6. Learn from his/her expertise
7. Best practices and methodology
8. Independence and objectivity
9. Confidentiality
10. Cultural affinity (in international M&As)

A third area of advantage is to be able to obtain from outside the skills needed for future M&A projects and transfer them to internal IT staff. The transfer of skills also includes best implementation practices and methodologies. Top consultants have typically very broad experience and inter-personal skills which can be utilised in many other subtle ways by the CIO. These can include communications with senior management, general and functional management, coaching and mentoring.

There are, therefore, good reasons why a consultant may sometimes be required and will add value. For example, a new project may be started that requires a particular expertise that is not available internally. Similarly unless a company has M&A as part of their continuous business development with a dedicated M&A IT team (such as Intel, Cisco, GE), most companies contemplate an M&A infrequently. These companies may lack available management resources as well as expertise and additional external help such as a good consultant is more than justified.

The M&A IT project is a complex affair. Timely execution of all the IT integration activities is a key success factor to insure that the M&A does not fail. The amount of planning, communications, detailed analysis of infrastructure, processes, skills and resources, development, testing and implementation of the systems integration routines and the understanding of the myriad of technical and management issues makes the IT M&A project particularly challenging. In this situation it seems more than justified to get all the help that one can. Typical reasons cited by companies for employing IT consultants in the IT M&A process are show in Box 12.2.

The disadvantages of using consultants

Companies fall into one of two categories: those that employ consultants and those that do not. A few years ago one of the authors worked for a very successful company that had a policy of not using external consultants. When asked why, the CEO stated 'I just don't believe they add any value'. This is a widely held view among companies that do not use consultants. McKay (2002) lists a range of negative comments clients make about consultants:

- are arrogant and egotistic
- discount the price to get in the door
- shape the demand for their services
- rubberstamp management decisions
- use senior consultants to win the contract and then use junior staff to complete the work

---

Box 12.2 CIO's comments on how to use consultants

- The use of external consultants was considered unnecessary in our case because we felt that we had the necessary skills in-house. However, the due diligence exercise failed to identify serious risks and in retrospect this may have been also a mistake. Having consultants that have done this type of exercise before is very valuable and avoids falling into traps that are difficult to avoid when one makes an acquisition for the first time. You need a forensic type of approach which is difficult to find in a normal IT Dept.
- Consultants are useful in situations where a discrete piece of work is required and has well defined boundaries, for example, a deployment of a Novel network with voice over IP capabilities or when advice on strategic options that consultants have experience from working with other clients. However, it is not a good idea for consultants to lead an M&A IT project. This should be always be done by a key figure of the client's staff.
- Our company has its own internal M&A IT consulting division therefore the use of consultants is kept relatively low and only used if specific technical skills or additional resources are required.
- External consultants were used in the implementation of the SAP ERP package but not in any other IT area during the acquisition process. We felt that our in-house M&A expertise in this area was sufficient.
- External IT consultants were not used during the first M&A work. We used an external third party in the second, but remained in control of the whole operation.
- We did not use consultants in our M&A project. However, in complicated M&A transactions it may be good to bring an interim IT Director to help with the management and integration issues.

- make recommendations that make them indispensable
- fail to understand the client's needs
- fail to deliver the results promised
- provide recommendations that are too complex to implement

The key disadvantages of using IT consultants are the cost and the perception that they do not add value. The cost alone should not be the deciding factor as this must be weighed against the costs of slower and poorer delivery of the M&A integration plan. Costs became an issue only when the quality of the consultant's work does not match the demands of the job.

Schiesser (2001) notes that the introduction of external consultants can affect employee morale negatively. Again, this drawback must be balanced against the advantages of securing additional resources at a critical time. However, resource constraints in IT departments and the demand for more IT people as a result of an increase in the volume of

M&A work may change this perception and make M&A IT consultants more in demand.

The consultant's role

IT Consultants can take on a variety of tasks and roles depending on the circumstances of the particular M&A. For example, working as an external IT consultant in a recent assignment for a client in the retail sector, one of the authors was brought in to play the role of Interim IT Director for their new subsidiary and develop and manage the IT post-acquisition integration. In another example the IT consultancy team worked alongside client staff and other consultants to provide the client with a successful post-acquisition integration and to achieve both IT and business synergies following the merger of two manufacturing groups.

There are plenty of other examples where companies have secured the services of a top name consultancy company that has provided all the necessary skills (including IT) to carry out all the pre-acquisition activities. For example, in the merger of two manufacturing groups consultants were brought in to facilitate the whole M&A process from the pre-acquisition stage to the full implementation and it was very successful. All the merger work was completed on time and the synergies and savings identified were higher than originally anticipated and thus the client was very satisfied with the outcome.

Some of the typical activities undertaken by the external IT consultant in M&A projects are shown in Box 12.3.

Pre-acquisition

The decision to use or not a consultant should be made at this point. Some companies, including the very experienced and the very inexperienced take a view up front that they will need consultants and identify

---

Box 12.3 Activities undertaken by an IT consultant

1. validating the M&A It integration approach
2. 'kick-starting' planning and assessment activities during the pre-close phase, e.g. carry-out IT due diligence
3. assisting IT management in the integration effort
4. transferring know-how, methodologies, tools and project management techniques including training
5. providing additional IT resources
6. launching rapid action items in order to achieve quick wins, reduce risks and achieve cost savings
7. providing specialised expertise in systems integration, change management and cultural alignment

the areas where they will use them. The majority start with the view that they do not need an external consultant or that they are going to see how far they can go with their own resources before making a call to a consultant. A second category has a policy of not using consultants and set off to do the entire M&A process on their own. This group tends to recruit additional M&A skills as part of their permanent staff *before* the M&A process starts.

We can get a useful insight into the role of the external IT consultant in this pre-acquisition phase by looking at the experiences of some of the companies discussed by the CIOs during the interviews.

The following three examples are where consultants were not used at the pre-acquisition stage and lack of internal expertise or experience led to problems later in the M&A. In the example of C1, P1 felt that an IT due diligence was not required. The disadvantages became apparent later: because no adequate assessment of IT risks was undertaken at the pre-acquisition stage there was a severe underestimation of the work-load in the post-acquisition stage that increased the interface costs and risks and delayed the project considerably. A similar situation happened in C2. Due diligence was done by the CIO who had never done this type of work before. He underestimated the cultural and technical issues to follow in the post-acquisition stage.

C3 involved two large multinationals who felt that they had plenty of their own IT resources to accomplish the merger. No external consultants were used but instead a new European IT Director who had accomplished M&A previously was recruited. He joined P3 once the merger had been announced and no formal IT due diligence was carried out. The result was a much longer and more difficult integration and additional costs.

Where there is sufficient internal expertise there may be no need for additional external resource. In C4 no external consultants were used at the pre-acquisition stage. Due diligence was carried out effectively by the internal IT team who had previous M&A experience and they helped to prepare the post-acquisition integration activities. By contrast in C5 an external IT consultant was used to carry out the due diligence. The rationale for using an external consultant was that neither P5 nor S5 were considered to have the relevant experience to undertake the M&A IT engagement and P5's CEO wanted an objective assessment of S5's IT capabilities.

Post-acquisition

The post-acquisition stage is where the need for using consultants is felt more acutely. At the pre-acquisition stage there are considerations such as low activity, uncertainty about the M&A transaction not progressing for a variety of reasons, and confidence in the company's own abilities and resources which militate against using consultants. When the deal has been announced the 'temperature rises' and it is then when people start thinking that perhaps they do not have all the capabilities, skills and resources internally that they thought they had.

The dilemmas that IT Directors and CIOs go through in deciding whether or not to bring an external consultant are illustrated in Box 12.4.

The case studies noted above demonstrate a marked difference between patterns of hiring consultants during the pre and post-acquisition phases.

C1 had considerable IT problems in the integration phase. There had been no due diligence and the integration strategy ran into many technical IT problems that took considerable time to resolve. As a result considerable external IT resources for data management, development and testing had to be added. An IT skills shortage at the time and the new technology employed, made it difficult to find the right IT consultants.

Box 12.4   Bringing in a consultant?– the IT director's dilemma

In a complex merger a few years ago where I had taken the position of It Director I was thinking whether I was going to be able to accomplish the work on time without extra help. At the beginning of the post-integration process, the supplier of the ERP software that the company was planning to roll-out came to me and said: 'Frank, I know someone that has just done this type of implementation and he would be very useful in your current situation. He is an external consultant, he is very good but he is expensive'. I checked his credentials and they were first rate, same as his fees. After considering the pros and cons I felt that I had a member in my IT team that although he clearly did not have the same experience as the proposed consultant I thought he could do the job. I thought I was making the right decision. Aftrer all, I thought I was saving company's money and using our own resources and at the same time giving an opportunity to a member of my own team. What could it be better? However, it was a few days later when I realized that the internal person could not accomplish the task and that the idea of using the external consultant did not seem such a bad idea after all. Luckily I was still able to hire him at slightly discounted fee than originally discussed. Without his expertise we could not have completed the project on time. The moral of the story: 'don't be put off by high fees'. After I was able to sell it to my boss as money saved rather than money spent because the costs of running the project late would have been much higher.

So, money is of relative value ... it is what you achieve with it that matters ...

Source: personal recollection by one of the authors.

Because the initial resource estimates and budgets did not anticipate anywhere near the level of external consultancy required, it was necessary to compromise the number and quality of the external resources utilised.

C2 did not use external resources at any stage. It decided to employ additional staff on a permanent basis instead. Three senior IT staff were brought in to add to the project management and international expertise that the company needed to achieve a successful IT integration. A subsequent review of the M&A suggested that the company could have benefited from an external consultant's expertise. External advice could have resulted in a clearer integration methodology and strategy that could have saved time and money and could have been used for other acquisitions that followed. In other aspects of the M&A consultants could have assisted the completion of a thorough technical assessment of the infrastructure of the companies that were acquired and merger benefit reviews. These would have made it easier to demonstrate the synergies achieved and adjust plans for further IT investment when the group IT strategy was reviewed three years later.

The merger of the two large companies in C3 used external IT consultants at the post-integration stage in a number of areas, mainly on project management, ERP technology and networking infrastructure. The consultants were attached to the specific integration teams working with the company's own internal IT staff and thus we were able to learn from them. With the benefit of hindsight consultants would have been helpful in relation to due diligence, technology assessment and integration, change management and business process optimisation. The parent company, which later made a number of other acquisitions, decided to set-up a dedicated M&A integration team and used many of the learning points and experiences from this merger.

The acquisition of S4 in C4 used several external IT consultants mainly in the areas of IT applications and business processes. A senior IT consultant was also used to interface between the acquired IT department and the integration IT team from the parent company. This worked well and softened the cultural and technical differences between parent and subsidiary. Without this role it would have been more difficult to find an acceptable compromise to resolve the business process and systems issues.

The acquisition of S5 in C5 relied heavily on the use of IT external consultants throughout the process. The acquired company was small and did not have the resources to undertake the integration. P5 had plenty of IS resources but incompatible IS skills with those of the acquired company and no previous M&A experience. In addition P5 management had adopted a hands-off approach to S5 and did not want S5's entrepreneurial spirit dented by the heavy tactics of P5's bureaucracy. External consultants provided the safety net and facilitated the cultural transition and IT roadmap to the integration with P5.

The interviews with CIOs confirmed that the majority of companies prefer to go it alone rather than use external IT consultants during an M&A project. Larger companies seem more likely to use consultants as a matter of course than small ones perhaps reflecting company policies and willingness to pay. Nevertheless, external consultants can be seen to play a vital role in supplying technical expertise and IT M&A know-how at key points in many transactions.

How to choose an IT M&A consultant

In order to be able to choose the right consultant it is necessary to prepare a brief description of the role, scope, objectives and the person profile before arranging to see the candidates. During the interview these details should be discussed fully as they provide a good tool for assessing the consultant's experience and suitability. In the example quoted in Box 12.4 a consultant was needed who could programme and manage the JD Edwards ERP system roll-out. The scope was to implement the ERP system in the first country. The primary objective was to implement it within a nine-month period. The secondary objective was that the consultant trained a member of the IT team who could then lead the implementation in subsequent sites.

Once the role, scope and key objectives have been defined the search is normally carried out through a mixture of formal and informal methods. For example, consultancy firms, hardware and software vendors and search firms are the traditional formal channels. Informal channels are personal networks and personal recommendations. Independent professional bodies such as The Institute of Management Consulting, British Computer Society or similar bodies offer free advice and they provide lists of qualified consultants for the particular requirement.

Selecting a big firm or small contractor is a question of the requirements, the budget and personal preference and experience. The maxim of 'never hire a big firm to do small jobs' applies here in the same way as for any other project. 'Free-lance consultants often offer the same experience and knowledge that you would get from a large firm but without the high overheads' (Wei 2002). On the other hand a complex international project involving multiple offices in several countries, with large and complex IT infrastructure may well benefit from the assistance of the big consulting firm.

After the interview the consultant should provide the CIO with a brief written proposal of how he/she intends to address the requirements. This document will show the experience and capability of the consultant or consultancy firm. Equally important is the personality and chemistry of the consultant to work along with the internal IT and business resources.

Before making the final decision the CIO should check the references and track record of the consultant to make sure that everything is in order. An area that often gets neglected is the question of whether the original consultant can be substituted or not by another consultant at any point during the engagement. Standard engagement contracts make substitution the norm. Unless the client agrees with the consultancy for this contract clause to be changed he or she may find that the original consultant that won the order may get changed

Before the consultant arrives the CIO should prepare his/her arrival and discuss the role, scope and reason for choosing a consultant with the internal team. Although this detail is perhaps seen as unnecessary it is essential to prepare the ground within the IT department(s) and within the business. Once the consultant is on board the CIO should introduce him/her to all the relevant parties in particular to the people that he/she will be working with and check that the chemistry is working well and to avoid potential conflict such as the one described in Box 12.5.

In a complex merger where the political climate is perhaps difficult care must be taken that the consultant is not used by one of the factions. In some mergers consultants 'can quickly become a lighting rod for politically based organisational differences by unintentionally disturbing an organisation's established political equilibrium' (Block 1981).

Box 12.5 Meeting the consultant before he or she arrives

A few years ago working as an independent consultanti in an internationa M&A project upon my arrival on the first day I was introduced to the IT manager that I was supposed to be working with. Although I had had a preliminary telephone discussion with him about my role before being offered the assignment we had not met.

It was a few days later after we started working out the details of what needed to be done that I realized that he was not happy. He expected me to do most of the work whereas I had been told by the CIO (the IT Manager's direct boss) that in order for the IT Manager to learn from me and have an effective transfer of skills we should share the tasks and work together. Clearly the CIO had not communicated that same message to his IT manager.

Source: personal recollection by one of the authors.

Once the consultant is on board it is important to receive regular updates to ensure that things are progressing according to plan. If the consultant is the right person he/she will welcome the opportunity of keeping the CIO informed and building a good rapport with him/her. In an M&A project the CIO's management time may be difficult to get but this is a key requirement. Regular updates also avoid the situation whereby sudden surprises appear at the end of the project. This is another reason for making sure that internal people are working closely with the consultant, as well as learning from his/her techniques. The final stage comes to when the implementation of the consultant's recommendations are tested. For this to be successful it is important to

---

Box 12.6 Do's

1. identify the needs early on in the M&A process
2. clearly define the objectives that you want to achieve
3. select the right consultant by researching the market or better by recommendations
4. match the experience of the consultant to your needs
5. check the consultant's credentials and track record
6. short-list no more than three consultants and ask them for brief written proposals
7. brief the consultant properly
8. meet the individual consultant who will do the job and ensure that the personal and team chemistry is right
9. ask for and follow references
10. agree the expectations in writing by means of a contract
11. be involved and in touch during the assignment
12. ensure that the consultant does not save surprises for the final stages of the project
13. maximize the consultant's experience by involving your staff in working with the consultant

---

Box 12.7 Don'ts

1. leave until it too late before calling a consultant
2. assume that the consultant understands your expectations unless you communicate them to him/her
3. use a consultant when you are not clear about the objectives
4. use a consultant for all the wrong reasons
5. assign your B team to work with the consultant
6. use the consultant as corporate referee
7. allow the consultant to plant his roots
8. neglect your own responsibility in the project

have the involvement of the internal resources. Apart from the final transfer of knowledge, it is essential that the ownership of the consultant's ideas and solutions remains in the company.

The work and research done by the client to find the right consultant is critical. 'If you've done a good job picking your consultants and using them, they'll deliver a return to your bottom line that's ten times what you laid out in cash. If you don't do your homework, however, expect to be taken for a long, unpleasant ride. And you'll deserve it too' (Lieber 1996). For the CIO faced with the need to acquire external expertise during an M&A there are a number of essential Do's and Don'ts that should be borne in mind. These are shown in Boxes 12.6 and 12.7.

13
Conclusions

The economic logic behind M&As is the notion of the creation of greater value through enlarged combined operations than could be achieved separately by the constituent companies or organisations. Anything that threatens the creation of such value must be regarded as a risk that should, if possible, be mitigated. IT is just such a factor: it can account for a very significant proportion of the synergies identified in an M&A. The ability of IT to deliver is central to the success of many M&A deals. Reducing the risks associated with IT systems and operations in an M&A is therefore vital for the overall success of the transaction.

The three ways of reducing IT risks

There are three main ways in which the risks associated with the IT side of the business can be reduced.

1. The IT function, normally through the CIO, needs to be involved in the M&A transaction from the start of the process. Problems relating to IT are best identified as soon as possible. The better informed the M&A team is about IT issues, and the better informed the CIO is about the business case and the target company; the better the decisions that will be taken about the deal and its implementation. Conversely, the later the involvement of the IT function and the consideration of IT issues, the greater the risks that IT problems that emerge will prevent the achievement of the expected synergies and the greater the likelihood of operational difficulties during and after the integration of the separate companies.
2. The CIO should already have a well-defined IT strategy in place covering systems, infrastructure, processes and people that is aligned to

the business strategy. A clear strategy helps the CIO to work systematically through the phases of a merger or acquisition from due diligence to assessment, integration and review. An IT department that is already experienced in effective identification of strategies and planning will avoid ad-hoc decisions that increase the risks of costly mistakes.

3. The CIO and his or her senior team need to possess or have access to a range of skills including experience of working in an M&A environment in order to handle the overall integration project effectively. Many of the risks involved in an M&A transaction attach to the management of the integration project itself. M&A IT projects are unconventional and demand very high levels of analysis, resource planning and implementation in the context of significant organisational change.

These three factors illustrate that reducing the risk associated with IT in a merger or acquisition is as much a matter of preparedness as of execution. A well-organised IT function with clear strategies and effective organisation and processes is in a much better position to tackle an M&A's requirement for quick decision making and adherence to very tight deadlines. The integration of the IT function in the combined organisation also depends on the application of best practices throughout the change process and effective leadership, communications and management. However, no amount of preparedness on the part of the CIO and the IT function will suffice if the deal itself is badly structured and unrealistic objectives and expectations are set for IT to deliver on.

The future

The challenges facing the CIO in the future in the shape of delivering value through M&A are likely to be as great or greater than at present. All indications are that the level of mergers and acquisition activity experienced in recent years will be at least sustained and may possibly continue to accelerate. In addition, more complex mergers and acquisitions are increasingly taking place. Complexity is illustrated when transactions cross national boundaries and those managing the integration have to deal with a different socio-legal and cultural framework. Complexity is also introduced by the complicated patterns of ownership and service provision that characterise both modern corporations but particularly the IT function. Over recent years many IT functions or parts of those functions have been out-sourced. In the context of the M&A deal the IT risks may be located in a third-party.

The increasingly central role of IT in the business also provides a growing challenge for senior management contemplating a merger or acquisition. It is now commonplace for all the key operations of an organisation to be dependent on IT. Companies rely on IT for production of goods and services, sales, delivery, accounts and virtually every aspect of their operations. IT, however, is no longer a purely internal, inward-facing factor but increasingly it is an outward-facing customer focused function. An IT failure can have immediate impact on the customer, who may no longer be able to order goods or services, track delivery or pay bills. IT problems have the ability to escalate very quickly through modern operations. While the CIO bears the responsibility for ensuring that IT runs smoothly and emerges from an M&A as an effective, integrated function, senior management needs to understand and support IT. Ignoring IT, failing to take account of the strategic role of IT within the business, and failing to support IT during the change process add unnecessarily to the risks inherent in a merger or acquisition.

In the book the discussion of the key issues facing the CIO was discussed with the aid of the BTM Model. The configuration of issues within the model varies between companies and between sectors. Over time the factors under each of these headings will also change. For example, it is likely that mergers and acquisition activity will become more commoditised and large companies will increasingly maintain permanent M&A teams and develop standard policies and procedures for handling such transactions and attendant integration issues. Other companies lacking such teams may increasingly look to external expertise to match such approaches. Another example already noted is the increased complexity of the M&As. M&As do not necessarily involve targeting independent companies or organisations. Often the target is part of another company. Such transactions mean that while one CIO will be planning integration, the management of the selling company including the CIO must be prepared to deal with divestment and uncoupling. This process poses its own issues of downsizing and management change.

From the technology viewpoint some trends are likely to make the IT integration easier. Convergent standards facilitated by consolidation of suppliers and changes in a more mature IT industry will reduce the incompatibility problems that have dogged M&As in the past. In some respects these developments will make the CIO's task easier. However, new challenges relating to obsolescence and replacement and the deployment of internet based technologies with associated organisational changes, continue to reinforce the need for clear strategies, planning and execution.

Managing the integration process will remain the CIO's main challenge in mergers and acquisitions. As indicated the challenge will come from many directions. There is an increasing likelihood that one or more of the parties to a transaction will have outsourced its IT emphasising the importance of contract management and negotiation skills. Increasing cross-border activity is likely to add more difficulty and management challenges as M&As cross more and different boundaries and CIOs have to work with companies in new regions. The complexity of M&A is growing, placing more demands on the CIO at a time when the M&A may have put his or her job on the line.

Whatever the nature and balance of issues relating to business, technology and management that emerge in a future M&A the CIO will need to work through the Phase Model using best practices. However, future challenges may alter some of the tasks to be carried out at different stages of the M&A and change their relative importance. More emphasis is likely to be placed on the role of due diligence as a result of Sarbanes-Oxley and other legal and accounting changes. Due diligence is likely to become a longer and more demanding process and put more demands on the CIO as IT assets and liabilities are investigated prior to the agreement of the M&A.

The counterpart of moving IT up the M&A agenda is likely to be the requirement for the CIO to conduct a more detailed assessment and to engage in more complex final planning processes. As part of this requirement the CIO will increasingly need to undertake formal risk assessment and sensitivity analysis on budgets and to utilise more sophisticated methodologies designed to analyse synergies and risks related to the IT function.

Finally, post-integration review is likely to become a more standard and formal part of the IT integration process. Greater M&A activity increases the importance of learning from experience and capturing this learning in a formal way. The increasing visibility of IT and the scale of synergies involved in many transactions means that formal review and performance cannot be overlooked.

Preparing to face the future

Change is a fact of corporate life that the CIO is better placed than many to understand because of the nature of IT. The change that may result from implementing new IT systems can impact significantly every business process and operation in the organisation. An M&A will also leave an imprint on every part of both the acquiring and the acquired organisation. Tackling the integration that follows an M&A is in essence just another change management project, but in reality one carried out in the most challenging circumstances that require fast effective working in an overstretched, potentially hostile and uncertain environment.

Nothing prepares a CIO for undertaking an M&A better than having done an M&A before. However, the interviews with CIOs suggested that the lessons that they had learned from the involvement in M&As are in many ways very simple. M&As require excellent planning, management and communications skills: M&As fail to deliver their objectives when they are poorly planned and poorly managed. An M&A may require the CIO to exercise his or her planning and management skills in the harshest of conditions, but success depends very greatly on building the capacity to plan, manage and influence. All of these skills can be acquired and developed on an ongoing basis so that when M&A is in the air they can be mobilised to ensure that IT maximises the opportunities offered by a takeover or merger and minimises the risks that may be involved.

Appendix I   Agenda Used During Interviews with CIOs

What has been your M&A experience as an IT director?

In relation to specific mergers or acquisitions identified:

* What M&A vision and strategy did the company have?
* At what point was IT involved in the M&A strategy?
* What was the role of IT during the acquisition?
* What contribution did IT make during the M&A process?
* How were the communications issues addressed?
* What were the cultural issues involved and how were they addressed?
* Was there an international dimension; if so how were issues of language, distance and environment addressed?
* Were consultants used; if so what was their contribution?

What are the key lessons you have learned from you M&A experience?

If you were to be involved in an M&A now, what would you do differently and why?

Note: The agenda, together with the objectives of the research were sent to the interviewees prior to the interview taking place. The author, who had been involved actively in the additional cases, used the same template to reflect on the experiences involved.

Appendix II

Reference has been made in the text to published material on the subject of M&A. The reader who wishes to explore writings on M&A further has a huge volume of material to draw on.

A very extensive annotated bibliography of academic materials is attached to Selim et al. (2002), which can be accessed by the Institute of Internal Auditors' website, *http://theiia.org*. The bibliography contains summaries of over 150 key books and journal articles covering all aspects of mergers, acquisitions and divestments.

Since the bibliography was completed M&A has continued to be the subject of a variety of writings. The available literature falls into various categories.

1. *Papers and articles that chronicle particular M&As and M&A activity in general.* Many of these are to be found in the press and on the Web. Recent examples include: Bank (2005), Huber and Hatfield (2004), Maitland (2004), Nuttall (2005), Singer and Karnitschnig (2005).
2. *General books and articles on M&A.* By far the largest Section of literature focuses on the financial dimensions of M&A activity, but some cover more managerial aspects of the topic. Research into managerial aspects of M&A published in academic journals often has a longer shelf-life than more topical reviews. Examples include: Cooper and Gregory (2003), David and Singh (1993), Gertsen *et al.* (1998), Hayes (2001), Hitt and Pisano (2004), Moren (2002).
3. Discussion of IT in M&A is mostly to be found in articles in technical and industry journals. A considerable amount of such material can also be accessed via the web. Recent examples include: Bently (2002), Evers (2001), Gurton (2000), Kubilus (2003).

Bank, D. (2005). 'Oracle Agrees to Acquire Siebel for $5.85 billion'. *Wall Street Journal*, 13 Sept., p. A1.

Bently, R. (2002). 'IT Key to Integration Success'. *Computer Weekly*, 31 Jan., p. 32.

Cooper, C. and A. Gregory (2003). *Advances in Mergers and Acquisitions*, Vol. 2, Elsevier.

David, K. and Singh, H. (1993). 'Acquisition Regimes: Managing Cultural Risks and Relative Deprivation in Corporate Acquisitions'. *International Review of Strategic Management*, 4, pp. 227–77.

Evers, L. (2001). 'Don't Put Money on Mergers Savings', *Network News*, 30 May.

Gertsen, M., Soderberg, A.M. and Torp, J.E. (1998). *Cultural Dimensions of International Mergers and Acquisitions*. Walter de Gruyter.

Gurton, A. (2000). 'Minimising Merger Pains'. *Computer Weekly*, 10 Feb., p. 20.

Hayes, J. (2001). 'Addressing Operational Issues and Human Factors in Mergers'. *Bank and Accounting & Finance Publications*, Euromoney Publications, Fall 2001, Vol. 15, Issue 1, pp. 38–44.

Huber, N. and Hadfield, W. (2004). 'Spanish Practices to Rule Abbey–Santander Deal'. *Computer Weekly*, 5 Oct.

Kubilus, N. (2003). 'Mergers: IT Disaster or IT Opportunity'. *Computerworld*, 22 Sept.

Maitland, A. (2004). 'Two Households – Both Alike in Dignity'. *Financial Times*, 12 Oct., Leadership Interview: Martin Read, CEO, Logica–CMG.

Moren, S. (2002). 'In Mergers, Convert Customers, Not Just Accounts'. *American Banker*, 28 Aug., Vol. 167, Issue 165, p. 9A.

Nuttall, C. (2005). 'An Acquisition Too Far Topples Leading Lady'. *Financial Times*, 10 Sept., p. 26.

Pablo, A.L. and Javidan, M. (2004). *'Mergers and Acquisitions: Creating Integrative Knowledge'* Blackwell.

Selim, G.M., Sudarsanam, S., and Lavine, M. (2002). *Mergers, Acquisitions, and Divestitures: Control and Audit Best Practices.* The Institute of Internal Auditors Research foundation, Altamonte Springs, Florida.

Singer, J. and Karnitschnig, M. (2005). 'Europe Gets Merger Mania'. *Wall Street Journal*, 9–11 Sept., pp. M1, M5.

Vowler, J. (2005). 'Understand Supplier Motives and Prepare Contracts to Protect Your IT After a Merger'. *Computer Weekly*, 15 Feb., p. 24.

Wooldridge, L. (2003). 'A Perfect Match: IT's Role in Mergers and Acquisitions'. *Smart Business*, CSC UK, February 2003 issue.

References

Alexander, D. and Rivett, A. (1998). 'A Sea of Words, a Sea of Troubles', *Journal of Management Consulting*, 10(1), 41.

Angwin, D. N. and Savill, B. (1997). 'Strategic Perspectives on European Cross-border Acqusitions: A View from Top European Executives', *European Management Journal*, 15 Apr., pp. 423–35.

Argyris, C. (2000) *Flawed Advice and the Management Trap: How Managers Can Know When They're Getting Good Advice and When They're Not'*. Oxford University Press.

Bergholz, H. (1999). 'Do More Than Fix My Company'. *Journal of Management Consulting*, 10(4) 29–33.

Block, P. (1981). *Flawless Consulting: A Guide to Getting Your Expertise Used*. Johannesburg: Pfeiffer & Company.

Burnice, M. R. (2002). 'Hiring Consultants During Organisation Change: Politics and Amalgamation'. *The Journal of Behavioural and Applied Management*, Winter, vol. 3(3), p. 231.

Bushko, D. and Raynor, M. (1999). 'Consulting Watch: The World from the Client's Side of the Negotiating Table'. *Journal of Management Consulting*, (10)3, 66–68.

Chang, A. and Ibbs, W. (1998). 'Development of Consultant Performance Measures for Design Projects'. *Project Management Journal*, (29)2, 39–54.

Child, J., Faulkner, D. and Pikethly, R. (2003). *The Management of International Acquisitions*. Oxford University Press, pp. 10–14, 27, 50–62.

Collins, T. (2005). 'Revenue Faces Bill of Tens of Millions to End PFI Deal'. *Computer Weekly*, 8 Feb.

Dupre, J. (1999). 'Do Consultants Really Practice What They Preach?'. *The Journal for Quality and Participation*, vol. 22, i5, 32–35.

Fincham, R. (1999). 'The Consultant–client Relationship: Critical Perspectives on the Management of Organizational Change'. *Journal of Management Studies*, 36(3), 335–52.

Fournier, R. (1999). 'Build for Business Innovation – Flexible, Standardized Enterprise Architectures Will Produce Several IT Benefits'. *Information Week*, 1 Nov., pp. 127–38.

Gadiesh, O. (Boston), Buchanan R. (London), Daniell M. (Zurich) and Ormiston C. (Singapore) (2002). 'Leading The Way To Successful Mergers'. *Journal of Business Strategy*, Mar. – Apr., pp. 12–17.

Gancel, C., Rodgers, I. and Raynaud, M. (2002). 'Successful Mergers, Acquisitions and Strategic Alliances: How to Bridge Corporate Cultures', Mc-Graw-Hill, p. 7, 23.

Gitelson, G. (2001). 'How the Cultural Trap Deepens in Cross-Border Deals'. *Merger & Acquisition Journal*, 1 Dec., p. 5.

Glyde, J. and McBride, M, (2000). 'Managing Mergers & Acquisitions', *IT Options during M&A Integration*, Section 8, Caspian Publishing, pp. 48–55.

Goodwin, C. (1999) 'Merging IT'. *Accountancy*, July, pp. 37–8.

192   *References*

Gulati, N. (2002). *Capturing Sustainable Merger Synergy by Optimizing your IT Infrastructure'*. IBM Global Services, p. 10.

Hoffman, T. (1999). 'Fleet Aims to Dodge Merger Potholes: Analysts Believe Bank Will Avoid Missteps That Have Plagued BANK ONE, First Union'. *Computerworld*, 13 Dec., pp. 22–4.

Hoffman, T. (2003). 'GM and Bank One Take Opposite Approaches to Outsourcing'. *Computerworld*, 10 Mar.

Hoffman, T. (2004). 'IT Outsourcing Could Be an Issue in Bank Merger'. *Computerworld*, 19 Jan.

Huber, N. (2004). 'Bank Merger Plans Questioned'. *Computer Weekly*, 17 Aug., p. 4.

IDC (2005). 'IDC Sees Healthy IT Growth Through 2009', News story by James Niccolai, *Computerworld*, 16 Aug. 2005.

Intel (2002). 'Managing IT During Mergers and Acquisitions', White Paper, Dec. 2002.

IPG Financial Results (2005). 'Recent News', IPG Corporate web site: *http://investors.interpublic.com*

Jones, G. (2005). *Multinationals and Global Capitalism*. Oxford University Press, Ch. 2, pp. 16–41.

Key Strategy (2003) 'Why Do Mergers Fail? What Can Be Done to Improve Their Chances of Success?' Jan., pp. 3, 9. *http://www.keystrategy.com/reports/mergers*

Kolb, D. (1984). *Experiential Learning*, Prentice Hall.

KPMG (2000). *Merger & Acquisition Integration: A Business Guide*. KPMG Consulting, p. 3.

Lee, S. (2003) *Global Acquisitions – Strategic Integration and the Human Factor*. Palgrave, pp. 189, 269.

Lieber, R. B. (1996). *Controlling Your Consultants*. Time Inc.

McDonald, D. D. (2003). 'Mergers and Acquisitions: What Executives Should Know About IT'. *Business Integration Journal*, July, pp. 38–40.

Mergers & Acquisition Review, 1st and 2nd Quarter 2005, *http://banker,thomsonib.com*

Mitchell, W. and Capron, L. (2003). 'Managing Acquisitions to Change and Survive', *European Business Forum*, pp. 1, 2, 4.

Muller-Stevens, G. (2001) Riding the Crest of a Wave. *Ambassador*, Mar. 2001.

Murdock, M. (1997). 'Who Ya Gonna Call?'. *InfoWorld*, 19(10), 59–60.

M&A Article (2005). 'Europe Outpaces US in Volume of Deals', *Financial Times*, 29 Sept.

Office of Government Commerce (OCG), 'Introduction to Prince2', *http://www.ogc.gov.uk/prince2/about_p2/about_intro.htm*

O'Shea, J. and Madigan, C. (1997). *Dangerous Company: The Consulting Powerhouses and Businesses They Save and Ruin*. New York: Times Business.

Pautler, Paul A. (2003). 'The Effects of Mergers and Post-Merger Integration: A Review of Business Consulting Literature' (draft). Bureau of Economics, Federal Trade Commission, pp. 4, 35.

Popovich, S. G. (2001). 'Meeting the Pressures to Accelerate IT Integration'. *Mergers & Acquisitions Journal*, 1 Dec.

Ranger, S. (2001). 'GSK Shows The IT Costs Of Mergers'. *Computing*, 31 May.

Ranger S. (2001a) 'IT Managers Left In The Dark On Mergers'. *Computing*, 25 May.

Roberts, J. (2004). '*The Modern Firm*'. Oxford University Press, p. 251.

Roythorn, P. (1997) 'The Not So Happy Truth About Mergers', *Computing*, 3 Dec.

Samuels, M. (2001). 'CIOs Left Out Of Merger Discussions', *Computing*, 20 Sept.

Samuels, M. (2005). 'The Insourcing Trend Is Bringing All Back Home', *Computing* 12 May.

Sartain, L. (1998). 'Why and How Southwest Airlines Uses Consultants'. *Journal of Management Consulting*, 10(2), 12–17.

Savill, B. and Wright, P. (2002). *Success Factors In Acquisitions*. PricewaterhouseCoopers.

Schiesser, R. (2001). *Hitting the Mark With Hired Guns*. Prentice Hall, 20 Aug.

Shapiro, E., Eccles, R. and Soske, T. (1993). 'Consulting: Has the Solution Become Part of the Problem?', *Sloan Management Review*, 34(4) 89–95.

Silverman, G. (2005). 'A Global Goal That Proved Elusive', *Financial Times*, 11 Oct., p. 14.

Starbuck, W. H. (1992). 'Learning by Knowledge Intensive Firms', *Journal of Management Studies*, 29(4), 713–40.

Strassmann, P. A. (2003). 'Mergers and the Myth of Synergy', *Computer Weekly*, 4 Aug.

Vermeulen, M. (2000). *European M&A Trends in IT Services in 2000*. BNP Paribas, Paris, p. 28.

Very, P. (2004). *The Management of Mergers & Acquisitions*, John Wiley & Sons, p. 134.

Vestring, T., King, B., Rouse, T. and Critchlow J. (2003). 'Merger Integration: Why "Soft Issues" Matter Most'. *European Business Forum*, p. 3.

Vielba, F. (1993). 'Systems Integration within Tioxide Group – MBA Project', Sept., Internal Company Document.

Vowler, J. (2003). 'How Two Airlines' Systems Became One'. *Computer Weekly*, 22 July.

Watson J. (2003) 'Bank Reaps Benefits of Integration Plan', *Computing*, 25 Sept., p. 18.

Wei, N. S. (2002). 'Practical Management: How to Select and Manage Environmental Consultants', 1 July. *http://www.pollutionengineering.com*

Yip, G. (2003), *Total Global Strategy II*, 2nd edn, Pearsons.

Index